Dining Down Memory Lane, Volume II

Also by Shelley Howell
Dining Down Memory Lane (2018)

Dining Down Memory Lane

VOLUME II

A Collection of Recipes from Baltimore's Classic
Restaurants of Yesteryear

Shelley Howell

Illustrations by Heather McCarthy

Baltimore Memory Lane Publishing, LLC

Towson, Maryland 21204

Printed in the United States of America

ISBN 978-0-578-74813-9 (paperback)

LCCN 2018910113

Book and cover design by FatCat Studios

This book is lovingly dedicated to the memory of my grandparents - Harley Walter Howell (1908 - 1979) and Geneva Engelmann Howell (1915 - 2001), to whom I am eternally grateful for the many amazing opportunities and experiences they bestowed upon me in my youth.

Contents

PART THREE: CRAB COOKING OLYMPICS: EAST - WEST CRAB FIGHT

A recipe that is not shared with others will soon be forgotten, but when it is shared, it will be enjoyed by generations to come.

Recipes

Since publishing *Dining Down Memory Lane* in late 2018, I have had the pleasure of meeting and connecting with many of my readers. They often ask where I got the recipes. The restaurants they came from have long been shuttered, so I couldn't rely on the establishments themselves as resources. One reason I began this labor of love was my inability to find any cookbooks published by the restaurants where these dishes were made. I decided I needed such a book, and so I wrote it.

I have enjoyed cooking for as long as I can remember. Over the years I have collected many recipes in the form of newspaper clippings, magazine tear sheets, handwritten recipe cards, online forums, and old cookbooks. Years ago, when my mother was downsizing, she gave me some of her best Maryland cookbooks -true vintage treasures! She even passed on her personal collection of decades-old *Gourmet* magazines. When I began writing *Dining Down Memory Lane* some of these served as resources.

Many of the recipes I found for *Volume II* came from further exploration of newspaper archives, with the vast majority coming from the *Baltimore Sun*. I also scoured second-hand thrift shops for vintage books and old copies of national food magazines, like *Bon Appétit*, whose columns often highlighted restaurant recipes their readers had requested. What a coup it was to find Haussner's recipe for *Wiener Schnitzel with Anchovies and Capers* submitted by Frances Haussner George herself! In the same vein, I found old community cookbooks to be particularly valuable sources. I even enjoyed watching an old episode of the *Food Network Challenge: Seafood Cook-Off*, a competition featuring chef Rudy Speckamp of Rudys' 2900 preparing his entry of *Soft Shell Crabs with Corn Relish, Field Greens and Roasted Red Pepper Sauce*.

These recipes all originated with the restaurants and bakeries. More than once, I was initially ecstatic to find a recipe for a "signature" dish, but upon further research found that it was only an unconfirmed version, and not an authentic recipe provided by the establishment. I chose not to include these. In the back of this book you will find a complete list of sources for the recipes here. Instructions for the recipes have been adapted in my own words, but the ingredient lists are exactly as I found them. A couple of the recipes call for MSG; when preparing those particular dishes at home, I either left it out altogether or made substitutions. I now invite you to try these recipes yourself and recapture the tastes and smells of the restaurants we once loved.

DRINKS
Creamsicle (Hersh's Orchard Inn) | *96*
Hot Buttered Rum (Brentwood Inn) | *91*

APPETIZERS (or first courses)
Antipasto Caldo (Dici Naz Velleggia) | *99*
Baked Herbed Oysters (Haussner's) | *23*
Crab Fluffs (Thompson's) | *81*
Crab Fritters (Hersh's Orchard Inn) | *95*
Oysters Florentine (Thompson's) | *83*
Oysters and Smithfield Ham á la (Haussner's) | *31*
"Paradise Lost" Oysters (Milton Inn) | *124*
Salmon Tartare (Rudys' 2900) | *137*
Toast Rudy (Capriccio) | *47*

SOUPS AND SALADS
Borscht (Harvey House) | *68*
Chicken Egg Drop Soup (New China Inn) | *74*
Crab Louis (Angelina's) | *161*
French Onion Soup (Harvey House) | *69*
Gazpacho (Hersh's Orchard Inn) | *94*
Green Bean Salad (Dici Naz Velleggia) | *102*
House Salad (Fiori) | *113*
Maryland Crabmeat Gumbo (Rudys' 2900) | *138*
Oyster Stew (Milton Inn) | *125*
Pumpkin Bisque with Crisp Ginger (Rudys' 2900) | *139*
Salade Eleanora (Milton Inn) | *126*
Seafood Sanibel (Rudys' 2900) | *140*
Strawberry Soup (Haussner's) | *36*
Tomato Florentine Soup (Haussner's) | *24*

DRESSINGS
Mayonnaise Dressing (Fiori) | *114*
Roquefort Dressing (Fiori) | *115*
House Vinaigrette (Milton Inn) | *126*

BREADS, PASTA, POTATOES & RICE
Fettuccine Carbonara (Rudys' 2900) | *147*
Garlic Bread (Maria's "300") | *42*

Linguine with White Clam Sauce (Fiori) | 115

Potato Dumplings (Haussner's) | 29

Rice Croquettes (Fiori) | 111

Rigatoni alla Vodka (Capriccio) | 48

Seasoned Lemon Rice (Haussner's) | 25

Spaetzle (Haussner's) | 27

Tyrolean Dumplings (Haussner's) | 30

ENTRÉES

Beef Braciola (Maria's "300") | 43

Beef Stir-Fry with Tomato (New China Inn) | 76

Boneless Breast of Pheasant Stuffed With Game Sausage
in Apple Brandy Sauce (Rudys' 2900) | 146

Butterfly Shrimp (New China Inn) | 75

California Crab Cornets (Angelina's) | 164

Calves' Liver with Bacon (Harvey House) | 70

Chicken Gismonda (Capriccio) | 50

Cornish Game Hens with Chestnuts (Country Fare Inn) | 108

Crab Brendan (Angelina's) | 163

Crab Cakes (Thompson's) | 80

Crab Cioppino (Angelina's) | 160

Crab Imperial (Miller Brothers) | 59

Crab Norfolk (the Broadview) | 165

Deviled Crab (Angelina's) | 162

Grilled Salmon Kabobs (Haussner's) | 25

Grouper and Salmon in Orange Fennel Butter (Rudys' 2900) | 142

Hasenpfeffer (Haussner's) | 26

Hungarian Goulash (Haussner's) | 28

Imperial Crab á la Maryland (Thompson's) | 157

Lobster Gratin with Green and White Asparagus (Rudys' 2900) | 145

Maryland Crab Cakes (Angelina's) | 158

Maryland Crab Cakes (Gordon's) | 156

Melini Veal Chop with White Bean Ragout (Milton Inn) | 127

Pan-Fried Rockfish with Crab Hash and Delmarva Salsa (Milton Inn) | 128

Paprika Schnitzel (Haussner's) | 32

Poor Man's Lobster (Winterling's) | 16

Pork Chops with Vinegar Peppers (Fiori) | 116

Roast Duck in Green Sauce (Country Fare Inn) | 107

Roasted Fresh Ham with Fruit and Herb Stuffing (Haussner's) | *33*

Rockfish Soufflé (Thompson's) | *82*

Saltimbocca alla Gino Marchetti (Dici Naz Velleggia) | *101*

Scallops Gauguin (Country Fare Inn) | *106*

Scampi (Capriccio) | *49*

Seafood Lord Calvert (Miller Brothers) | *60*

Seared Rockfish with Oyster and Corn Stew (Rudys' 2900) | *141*

Shrimp Scampi (Thompson's) | *84*

Soft Shell Crabs with Corn Relish, Field Greens
and Roasted Red Pepper Sauce (Rudys' 2900) | *143*

Southern Fried Chicken á la Maryland (Miller Brothers) | *58*

Steaks "the old-fashioned way" (House of Welsh) | *64*

Swiss Steaks (Winterling's) | *17*

Veal Scallops with Mozzarella and Prosciutto (Capriccio) | *51*

Weiner Schnitzel with Anchovies and Capers (Haussner's) | *34*

SAUCES

Blueberry Ketchup (Milton Inn) | *130*

Beurre Blanc (Milton Inn) | *124*

Cranberry Relish (Milton Inn) | *131*

Curry Sauce (Hersh's Orchard Inn) | *95*

Marinara Sauce (Fiori) | *112*

Roasted Red Pepper Sauce (Rudys' 2900) | *144*

VEGETABLES

Fried Eggplant (Haussner's) | *35*

Green Beans Margherita (Fiori) | *117*

Roasted Parsnip Purée (Rudys' 2900) | *148*

Tomatoes Mentonnaise (Country Fare Inn) | *105*

DESSERTS

Apple Crumb Pie (Winterling's) | *18*

Chocolate Cake (Doebereiner's) | *2*

Chocolate Marble Terrine (Milton Inn) | *132*

Chocolate Sabayon (Fiori) | *118*

Chocolate Walnut Pastry (Ms. Desserts) | *6*

Chocolate Zucchini Cake (Ms. Desserts) | *7*

Homemade Rice Pudding (Harvey House) | *70*

Honey Cake (Silber's) | *11*

Preface

Nothing brings people together like good food. Growing up in a small close-knit family, my childhood was influenced significantly by my paternal grandparents who lived only a short distance from us. Sunday dinners at their Lutherville home was a long-standing tradition that my sisters and I looked forward to. On special occasions, dining at fine restaurants was often a part of the celebration. My grandparents introduced my sisters and me to such establishments as the Chesapeake, the Tail of the Fox (later known as Shane's), Peerce's Plantation, and the Orchard Inn. This gave us an opportunity to wear our finery, practice our manners, and try different foods. They encouraged our presence, forging a connection with their grandchildren that was of primary importance to them.

Dining Down Memory Lane evolved because the restaurants and recipes I described there remind me of special times shared with family and friends. Those memories are bittersweet...bitter because they were shared with people no longer with us. They were sweet, because they were happy times I could recreate in my mind over and over. The thought that those memories could one day fade into oblivion did not sit well with me. I tend to romanticize things that are no longer there - the "absence makes the heart grow fonder" factor. These memories need to be preserved, and that's what this book is all about.

For as long as I can remember I have enjoyed collecting recipes of all sorts. The evolution of *Dining Down Memory Lane* began one rainy Wednesday morning in 2006. Still sipping coffee in my robe and pajamas, as I perused the *Baltimore Sun*, I came across a reader's request for the recipe for Haussner's Strawberry Pie. Excitedly, I realized I had the very recipe in my collection and submitted it to the Sun where it was published on July 12, 2006. As I continued to explore the Recipe Finder column, I realized how much demand there was for recipes from restaurants of yesteryear. It was a new, impressive idea for me. Then, when Sun restaurant critic, Elizabeth Large wrote her blog on the topic of the *Top Ten Restaurants We Miss Terribly*, I concluded that I was not alone in my interest. I decided to write a book about past restaurants and their recipes. To be able to write with more feeling, I decided to include only restaurants in Baltimore City and County which I had personally experienced in my first book, *Dining Down Memory Lane*. It was never intended to be a completely comprehensive collection of defunct Baltimore restaurants.

While initially, the recipes were my singular interest, as I learned more about the histories of the restaurants, this piqued my curiosity. I became so consumed that I wanted to share my enthusiasm with fellow Baltimoreans, both current and former. I wanted to connect with others who shared fond memories of favorite restaurants gone-by, and their signature dishes.

Since the release of *Dining Down Memory Lane*, I have had the enormous pleasure of meeting many of my readers at area signings and book talks.

Others have connected with me by Facebook, e-mail, even handwritten notes and letters. People have shared so many wonderful heartfelt memories and stories with me. It has been an incredible experience to say the least. Many of you thanked me for writing it and asked me if I was planning to write another book. Thank you for the ultimate in compliments! Your suggestions for restaurant inclusions were duly noted and I have included many here in *Dining Down Memory Lane, Volume II*. I personally experienced dining at most of the restaurants in *Volume II*, but not all. Some, like Miller Brothers, reach too far back for me to remember. But I wanted to know more about the places my grandparents' generation frequented, and I soon learned some of their fascinating histories. I asked family and friends to share their recollections with me so that I could present the establishments with their perspectives in mind.

Our journey begins as I take you through neighborhoods from south to north, with stops at some of Baltimore's most iconic landmark restaurants of days gone by. I want this book to serve as the inspiration and vehicle that transports you, dear reader, on your own journey and to your own place of nostalgia, just as I experienced mine when writing *Dining Down Memory Lane*.

As I searched the archives for restaurant recipes, I had the good fortune of finding a few vintage bakery recipes too. These old Baltimore bakeries represented different nationalities. Each had its own "secret" family recipes that were rarely shared. I am pleased to include those findings here. Additionally, Part Three contains a bonus of sorts - some serendipitous crab dish finds that I hope you will enjoy. Here you'll find stories and mementos, recipes, and images that might spark old memories that truly matter. Although these beloved eateries relied upon a certain sense of style that reflected the times, their recipes live on, an enduring legacy of Baltimore's culinary history.

They say if you are going to write a book, write about something you enjoy. I've been fortunate to do that. It also takes a village and there are many people I'd like to thank for their time, talent and effort. This book would have been a lot less enjoyable to write without the direct and indirect help of the following people: Anna Aladiev, Mike Barth, Barb Clapp, Jim Considine, Margie Cronhardt, Mary Tilghman Dushel (Linthicum Library), Jaymee Farinacci (Friends of Perry Hall Library), Jennifer Franciotti (WBAL-TV), Haswell M. Franklin, Sr., Jennifer Freimund, M.D., Patricia Gould (Brightwood Living), Joyce Griffin (Women's Club of Roland Park), Emily Howell, Rebecca Howell, Carol Townsend Jones, Jacques Kelly (Baltimore Sun), Amanda Krotki and Richard Gorelick (Jmore), Diane Howell Mitchell, Meg Schwartzman Schudel, Judy Tormey Schwartzman, Amy Simon and Leslie Udoff (Eddie's of Roland Park), Leslie Greenly Smith (Harford County Public Library), Kim Solloway (Women's Club of Linthicum), Pat Thomas and not least, Cindy Wolf (North Oaks). This book would not have happened without all of you.

Without the resources of the *Baltimore Sun* family, past and present, I wouldn't have had half the information for this book.

To my creative team at FatCat Studios, thank you for bringing this book to life with imagery, art and illustration. Valentia McVey, without your expert direction and talent, this book wouldn't be as stylish or fun to look at. For the wonderful illustrations, I give heartfelt thanks to Heather McCarthy.

To Bear Press Editorial Services, thank you for helping to make this manuscript perfect and keeping my voice in the process.

To my mother Ann, thank you for gathering us around the dining room table at mealtime every night and setting such a great example of a now fading tradition. Growing up I just assumed every family did that. I have such appreciation for the lengths you went to, serving up healthy and delicious homemade meals, teaching me table manners and most of all, providing me with a lifetime of cherished family memories.

Lastly, a special thank-you to my partner in life, James "Mac" McKay, for your love, support and encouragement. You are the real deal.

Shelley Howell
June 2020

PART ONE: THE BAKERIES

Doebereiner's

Headquarters: 29 East North Avenue

Founder: George Doebereiner

Open: **1897 - 1953**

*I*n 1921 the Old Goucher college campus was still located at St. Paul and 23rd, right around the corner from Doebereiner's Confectioner on North Avenue. Goucher had a girls' sorority known as "Eta Bita Gu." The late Raymond L. Hughes, nephew of the last of the founding Doebereiners, thought it might be a reference to the nickname the girls gave the rich mocha cake, "Doeby's Gu."

Wedding Cakes
that are *different*
for the June Bride

Made of pound or lady cake. In tiers or in individual boxes with ribbon decoration.

Prizes range from $5.00 to $50.00.

Fancy Ices for the reception in hearts, flowers and slippers.

George Doebereiner
29 East North Ave.

Vernon 3110

Doebereiner's Chocolate Cake

Makes one 8" three layer cake

+ **1 ½ cups** sugar, divided
+ **½ cup** unsalted butter, softened
+ **2 eggs**, separated
+ **2 cups** flour

+ **1 teaspoon** baking soda (dissolved in a little water)
+ **1 teaspoon** vanilla
+ *Frosting*, recipe follows

Preheat oven to 350°F. Combine 1 cup milk and baking chocolate in a medium saucepan and heat on low until chocolate is melted. Stir in 1 cup sugar and bring to a boil. Boil until thick and syrupy, stirring occasionally, about 5 minutes. Set aside and allow to cool. In a large bowl cream together ½ cup butter and remaining ½ cup sugar until light and fluffy. Add egg yolks then add ½ cup flour, beating until smooth. Add the dissolved baking soda, cooled chocolate mixture and vanilla. Mix until fully incorporated. In a separate medium bowl beat the egg whites until stiff, then gently fold them into the mixture. Divide the batter evenly between three 8-inch round greased and floured cake pans.

Bake for 20 minutes or until tester comes out clean. Cool on wire rack for 5 minutes then remove from pans. Allow to cool completely before frosting.

Frosting

+ **16 ounces** powdered sugar
+ **½ cup** unsalted butter, softened
+ **6 teaspoons** cocoa powder
+ **1 teaspoon** vanilla

+ **¼ teaspoon** cinnamon
+ **¼ teaspoon** salt
+ **4 to 6 tablespoons** strong hot coffee
+ **¼ cup** slivered almonds
+ **2 tablespoons** butter

For the frosting, cream together the powdered sugar, butter, cocoa powder, vanilla, cinnamon, and salt until smooth. Add enough hot coffee to make the mixture a smooth, spreadable consistency. Cover layers and sides of cake with frosting. Toast slivered almonds in melted butter. Cool and sprinkle over top of cake.

Hutzler's Bakery

Headquarters: Saratoga Street

Founder: Abram G. Hutzler

Open: 1858 - 1990

After sampling fudge in Baltimore long ago, a Vassar student was inspired to make her own right in her dorm room. Snacking was considered taboo and a violation of school rules. The fad caught on, and later Smith College and Wellesley College both developed their own recipes for fudge. In 1898 two resourceful Wellesley graduates created a double fudge cake for the Wellesley Tea Room; the Wellesley fudge cake has been famous ever since. This recipe from the Hutzler's bakery was shared with the *Evening Sun* courtesy of Hannah Mazo, Hutzler's personnel manager, who copied the recipe from the store bakery before it closed. Way to go, Hannah!

Hutzler's - Wellesley Fudge Cake

Makes two 9"x 9" square cakes (cakes freeze very well)

- 2 **cups** butter
- 6 **cups** sugar
- 12 eggs
- 1 **quart** buttermilk
- ¾ **teaspoon** baking soda
- 7 ½ **cups** cake flour
- ½ **pound** melted bitter chocolate
- ½ **teaspoon** vanilla
- Chopped pecans
- *Chocolate Icing*, recipe follows

Preheat oven to 350°F. Cream the butter and sugar, add eggs, vanilla extract and set aside. Mix buttermilk and baking soda together – then add alternately with flour to the butter mixture. Pour in melted chocolate and mix thoroughly. (Note: The recipe says to add chopped pecans to batter but does not say how much or when to add.)

Pour batter into prepared 9x9-inch square cake pans. Bake until cooked through, about 20 to 25 minutes. Ice cake with chocolate icing.

Chocolate Icing

- 2 ½ **ounces** butter
- 1 ½ **ounces (3/8 cup)** bitter chocolate
- 3 **cups** confectioner's sugar
- 12 **ounces (1 ½ cups)** canned evaporated milk
- ½ **teaspoon** vanilla
- Chopped pecans for garnish

Melt butter and chocolate together. In a separate bowl, mix the confectioner's sugar, milk, and sugar together. Add the melted chocolate and butter. Mix thoroughly. Spread on the cake while the icing is still slightly warm. Sprinkle with chopped pecans.

Ms. Desserts

"No preservatives; no junk"

Headquarters: Harborplace; Light Street Pavilion

Founder: Dean Kolstad

Open: 1980 - 1992

*B*efore the chains took over Harborplace there was a Baltimore-based bakery known as Ms. Desserts. In addition to its sole retail store, Ms. Desserts products were sold to many area restaurants. What gave them the competitive edge? According to Ms. Kolstad in 1983, it was butter of higher quality and cost produced in the upper Midwest. These recipes were her personal specialties.

Chocolate Walnut Pastry

Makes 1 pastry

Pâte Brisée (pie dough):

+ **3 ½ cups** flour
+ **2 ¾ sticks** butter
+ **¼ cup** sugar
+ **2 eggs**
+ Ice water

In an electric mixer bowl, cut up butter; mix in flour and sugar until it becomes crumbly. Place eggs in a large measuring cup, adding enough ice water to reach the 2-cup mark. Add liquid all at once to dry ingredients, mixing a few seconds until combined. Wrap in plastic wrap and chill. When well chilled, roll out as for pie crust and fit into a greased 11-inch tart pan. Reserve extra dough. Return to refrigerator while preparing filling.

Honey Walnut Pastry Filling:

+ **1 ½ cups** sugar
+ **½ cup** water
+ **3 ½ cups** walnuts, plus extra walnut halves for decoration
+ **14 tablespoons** milk (one cup, less 2 tablespoons)
+ **14 tablespoons** butter (1¾ sticks)
+ **1/3 cup** honey

Preheat oven to 400°F. Caramelize sugar and water in heavy saucepan. Heat slowly until sugar dissolves, then boil over high heat until a deep golden brown. Carefully add nuts, milk, and butter all at once with heat off. Stir to combine, and then return to heat and bring back to a boil. Allow mixture to simmer for 15 minutes, stirring occasionally to prevent mixture sticking to pan. Remove from heat and stir in honey. Allow to cool for 15 minutes. While mixture is cooling, roll out top crust. Remove tart pan from refrigerator. Pour in filling. Place top crust over filling and crimp to completely seal. Cut a few slits to allow steam to escape and bake in preheated oven for 20 minutes or until golden. Cool and refrigerate at least 4 hours before icing.

Honey Walnut Chocolate Icing:

+ **8 ounces** chocolate chips
+ **½ stick** butter
+ **1 teaspoon** oil

Melt chocolate in a double boiler over simmering water. Add butter and oil, stirring until smooth and shiny. Spread while still warm. Garnish with reserved walnut halves

Chocolate Zucchini Cake

Makes 1 Bundt cake

- ½ **cup** walnuts
- 2 ½ **cups** flour
- ½ **cup** cocoa powder
- 2 ½ **teaspoons** baking powder
- 1 ½ **teaspoons** baking soda
- 1 **teaspoon** salt
- 1 **teaspoon** cinnamon
- ¾ **cup** butter
- 2 **cups** sugar
- 3 eggs
- 2 **teaspoons** vanilla
- 2 **teaspoons** freshly grated orange peel
- 2 **cups** zucchini, grated and drained of excess liquid
- ½ **cup** buttermilk
- *Cocoa Orange Frosting*, recipe follows

Preheat oven to 325°F. Combine flour, cocoa powder, baking powder, salt, baking soda and cinnamon, and set aside. Beat butter and sugar until creamy. Add eggs, one at a time, then vanilla, orange, zucchini and buttermilk. Then mix with dry ingredients, stirring until well blended. Stir in nuts. Pour batter into greased and floured Bundt or tube pan. Bake in preheated oven for 1 hour or until cake springs back. Allow to cool completely and frost with Cocoa Orange Frosting.

Cocoa Orange Frosting:

- 4 **tablespoons** butter
- 2 **cups** powdered sugar
- 3 ½ **tablespoons** milk
- 4 **tablespoons** cocoa powder
- 1 **teaspoon** freshly grated orange peel
- 1 **teaspoon** vanilla

Cream butter and sugar. Add cocoa powder and beat until well blended. Beat in milk, orange peel, and vanilla.

Rice's Bakery

Headquarters: Gay Street

Founder: Duane Rice

Open: 1868 - 1974

Rice's Bakery delivered to the doors of Baltimoreans for over 100 years. Before trucks, this door-to-door service was delivered by horse and wagon! An all-time Maryland favorite, Rice's famous Louisiana Ring Cake has a most delicious crunchy outer crust and a moist cake interior.

Louisiana Ring Cake

Serves 10 to 12 (one 10 to 12-cup tube pan)

Batter:

+ **2 ¾ cups** flour
+ **½ teaspoon** salt
+ **2 teaspoons** baking powder
+ **1 ¾ cups** sugar
+ **1 cup** shortening
+ **¾ cup** milk
+ **1 teaspoon** orange extract
+ **¼ teaspoon** almond extract
+ **3 eggs**, unbeaten
+ *Topping*, recipe follows

Preheat oven to 375°F. Grease and flour 10 to 12 cup tube pan. Sift flour, baking powder and salt into a large mixing bowl. Add sugar and blend. Cut in shortening (like making pie crust dough). Add milk, extracts and eggs. Beat thoroughly and set aside.

Topping:

+ **¾ cup** batter
+ **2 tablespoons** flour
+ **3 tablespoons** brown sugar
+ **3 tablespoons** powdered sugar
+ **¼ teaspoon** orange extract
+ **½ cup** chopped pecans (optional)
+ **½ teaspoon** grated orange peel (optional)

To prepare topping: Take ¾ cup of reserved batter and add flour, sugars, extract, chopped nuts and orange peel (if using). Mix well. Spread topping in bottom of prepared tube pan. Pour remaining batter on top. Bake in preheated oven for 45 minutes to an hour or until cake tester comes out clean. Remove from pan immediately or topping will stick. Allow coffee cake to cool before serving.

Silber's Bakery

Headquartered: 1313 East Lombard Street

Founders: Isaac and Dora Silber

Open: 1 9 0 7 - 1 9 8 0

$\int$ ilber's bakery was a beloved Baltimore institution with thirty-six stores that turned out amazing freshly baked goods every day. I have such fond memories of this sorely missed iconic bakery. Silber's recipes were produced in 100-pound batches, so it's a rarity to find an authentic recipe adaptable for home use. Fortunately, Mrs. Dora Silber shared some of her personal treasured Hanukkah recipes with the Sun in 1971.

Mandel Bread

A traditional Jewish cookie similar to biscotti

+ 5 eggs, beaten
+ **1 cup** sugar
+ **1 cup** shortening
+ **3 ½ cups** flour

+ **1 teaspoon** salt
+ **3 teaspoons** baking powder
+ Rind and juice of 1 orange
+ **¼ cup** nuts

Preheat oven to 350°F. Cream shortening and sugar. Add eggs and mix well. Sift flour, baking powder and salt. Add alternately to mixture with orange rind, juice and nuts. Spoon dough on a greased baking sheet in six strips and bake for 25 to 30 minutes, or until lightly golden. Allow to cool. Cut into ½-inch slices and toast in oven at 350°F for 5 minutes.

Honey Cake

Makes 1 tube cake or 2 loaf pans

+ **1 ½ pounds** honey (medium in color)
+ **1 cup** sugar
+ **¼ cup** cooking oil
+ **½ cup** strong coffee
+ **3 cups** flour
+ **1 teaspoon** baking soda

+ **1 ½ teaspoons** baking powder
+ **1 teaspoon** salt
+ **1 teaspoon** ground ginger
+ **½ teaspoon** allspice
+ **1 teaspoon** nutmeg
+ **2 tablespoons** rum

Preheat oven to 300°F. Combine honey and sugar. Stir in oil. Sift flour with baking soda, baking powder, salt and spices. Alternate adding flour with coffee to the honey mixture, beating well. Stir in rum. Bake in prepared pan(s) for 1 hour or until done.

PART TWO: THE RESTAURANTS

The House of Winterling

Neighborhood: Canton

3200 Foster Avenue

Open: 1923 - 1988

A Canton tradition - The House of Winterling was a place to meet, a place to eat. A quintessential, old-fashioned, East Baltimore, family-run, neighborhood restaurant, the kind Baltimoreans loved, in part because it never changed. It was a reliable oldie but goodie that offered fresh food in an immaculate setting at reasonable prices.

The corner restaurant comprised two row homes in a quiet residential section. When Leo "Skip" Winterling bought the second home in 1958 he came up with the idea of people relaxing in a "homey" environment, and designed it with that in mind: a place where you could get a homemade meal like mom used to make. The front part of Winterling's was divided between a bar and a sitting area, and the back part was two dining rooms that could accommodate 60 diners. To enter the main dining room, you passed through the sitting room which resembled a living room complete with sofas, wall paintings, hanging plants and a grandfather clock. Some of you might recall the royal blue wall-to-wall carpeting patterned with enormous unicorn heads, and the stairway off one of the dining rooms that led to the family living quarters. Mirrored arches were utilized to achieve a more spacious atmosphere and reflected the pristine tables set with fresh, white, linen tablecloths and "Queen Anne" high-backed chairs.

Mr. Winterling worked alongside his mother, Mary Ann. "Mrs. W" was famous for her house specialty sauerbraten (sour beef), an old family recipe that required two days of marinating. She was still preparing the sauerbraten until she was 80 and remained active in the kitchen well into her 80s. In later years, the kitchen duties fell to Skip Winterling's daughter and co-owner, Leah Bark, who faithfully followed the same recipes.

Winterling's was around for a long time and well known throughout the city. People came from all around to eat Maryland seafood and "Mrs. W.'s" sauerbraten. Although some thought of Winterling's as German, the menu was classic American and mostly devoted to seafood, except for sauerbraten and dumplings and "a touch of Old Erin," corned beef or ham and cabbage. Customers loved the rich lobster bisque, fresh red snapper or stuffed flounder, fried Maryland soft shell clams, standard crab dishes, steaks and pot roast too. Among the patrons having lunch on any day, you might have caught a glimpse of Jerry Hoffberger of National beer, or sports announcers Chuck Thompson and Charlie Eckman. Friendly waitresses delivered bread baskets of homemade yeast rolls and warm, golden blueberry muffins that came with the first course. Dinner entrées included a choice of two vegetables or a vegetable and salad with a long list of selections to choose from: fried eggplant, sweet and sour red cabbage, mashed potatoes, Silver Queen corn on the cob, stewed tomatoes, pickled beets and potato salad. Homemade desserts were not to be missed either! Winterling's had a reputation for its huge slices of fresh house-made pies and cakes temptingly presented on a tray by the waitress station. Selections often included German chocolate cake, deep dish cheesecake "pie," pecan pie, peach pie and the house specialty, apple crumb pie.

The House of Winterling never accepted credit cards, even when other restaurants like Haussner's finally succumbed to the practice. It remained true to its traditions for over 60 years, a reminder of another age, and was the kind of restaurant you wish you had in your own neighborhood.

Poor Man's Lobster

This is so easy to prepare, and the flavor is truly reminiscent of broiled lobster.

Serves 2

+ **1 pound** haddock filets partially thawed
+ **1 ½ cups** water
+ **1 ½ teaspoons** seafood seasoning
+ **1 ½ teaspoons** whole peppercorns
+ **1** bay leaf
+ **1** lemon, sliced
+ **1** stalk celery, chopped
+ **1** small onion, sliced
+ Melted butter
+ Paprika
+ *Lemon Butter Sauce*, recipe follows

In a 3-quart saucepan, combine water, seasoning, peppercorns, bay leaf, lemon, celery and onion. Simmer for 10 minutes. Cut fish into bite size pieces and add to simmering water. Cook for 8 minutes. Remove and place on a broiling pan. Brush with melted butter and broil 4 inches from heat source for about 5 minutes. Serve with lemon butter sauce.

Lemon Butter Sauce:

+ **½ cup** melted butter
+ Salt and pepper, to taste
+ Juice of **2** lemons
+ **2 tablespoons** breadcrumbs, optional

Mix all ingredients and serve on any broiled fish, lobster or shrimp.

Winterling's Swiss Steaks

Not much is known about the origins of Swiss steak, but the name may come from the English term, swissing, a method of smoothing cloth flat by rolling and pounding. Swiss steak became popular in the postwar '40s as an alternative to more spendy cuts of beef.

Serves 4

+ **4 8-ounce** pieces of eye round steak, ¾" thick
+ Flour, salt, pepper
+ **½ cup** oil
+ **2** medium onions
+ **2** medium peppers
+ **2** large cans whole tomatoes

+ **½ cup** sugar
+ **1 teaspoon** salt
+ **½ teaspoon** pepper
+ **1 teaspoon** oregano
+ **2 cups** water

Preheat oven to 350°F. Heat oil in a heavy skillet. Season steaks with salt and pepper and dredge in flour. Fry until brown on both sides. Place in a baking pan fitted with cover. Slice one onion and one pepper into 4 rings. Place one of each on each steak. Place 1 whole tomato in the center of onion and pepper rings. Set aside.

For the sauce:

Chop remaining onion and pepper and combine with 2 cans tomatoes (hand crushed). Add sugar, salt, pepper and oregano. Cook over low heat until sauce reaches a boil. Take ¼ of sauce and pour into baking pan around steaks with 2 cups water. Cover and bake steaks for about 2 hours or until tender. Check occasionally so liquid does not burn off. Simmer remaining sauce about 20 minutes longer. Set aside. Reheat and pour over steaks when ready to serve.

Apple Crumb Pie

Massive slices of extraordinary homemade pies were the only way to close out a meal at Winterling's. The crumb topping on this pie cooks together in the oven and turns into a crunchy layer on top of perfectly cooked apples. It's sure to have everyone raving!

Makes one 10" pie

+ **5 pounds** apples
+ **½ cup** sugar
+ **2 tablespoons** flour
+ **1 teaspoon** cinnamon
+ **1 10"** pie shell

Topping:

+ **¼ pound** butter
+ **2 cups** flour
+ **2 cups** sugar
+ **2 teaspoons** cinnamon

Preheat oven to 425°F. Peel, core and slice apples. In a large bowl, mix sugar, flour and cinnamon together and combine with apple slices. Place into unbaked crust with apples mounded higher in the center. For topping, melt butter in saucepan and add remaining ingredients. Toss with a spoon until crumb mixture forms. Cover apples completely with crumbs. Bake in preheated oven for 15 minutes. Reduce oven temperature to 350° and bake for another hour.

Haussner's Restaurant

"Famous for Fine Food and Fine Art"

Neighborhood: Highlandtown

3244 Eastern Avenue

Open: 1926 - 1999

"Oh, if only I could go back one more time...Can you believe it's been 20 years today that Haussner's officially closed their doors forever?" That is how I began my Facebook post on October 6th, 2019, a tribute to the late, legendary Baltimore institution that was Haussner's. Not surprisingly, I received a tremendous outpouring of response. So much a part of the Baltimore experience, it was equally popular a dining choice among visitors and natives alike. Here are just a few comments my post generated:

Sue - "My sister and I stood in the rain the last week they were open, just for one last Haussner's meal. I always ordered fried eggplant and mushroom crab imperial. Very special place."

Willa (who worked there from '85 - '91) - "It was a cool place to work. Mrs. H was angelic. She gave us a large painting for a wedding gift. She was one of a kind."

Diane - "Beautiful memories of a special time in a different era."

Indeed, a lost, golden age.

Haussner's was one of Baltimore's proudest success stories. Owned and operated by the Haussner family for seventy-three years, this local restaurant achieved national renown for its cuisine and massive art collection, becoming one of Baltimore's most famous landmarks. William Henry Haussner (1894-1963) and his wife, Frances Wilke Haussner (1909-2000) were partners in all things from the day of their marriage in 1935.

The couple amassed their huge collection of 19th-century European Academic and American paintings during the late 1930s and 1940s. Mrs. Haussner enjoyed attending auctions and encouraged her once initially reluctant husband to join her in collecting. He became as passionate as she was, and the result was an amazing collection of original paintings including works by Rembrandt, Whistler, de Blaas, Bierstadt, Gainsborough, Schreyer and Alma-Tadema, to name a few. Wisely, the couple bought art that they loved, but had gone out of vogue and was considered old-fashioned in its appeal.

They often purchased huge canvases with gilt frames and heavy marble statues that could only be accommodated by large houses of the day. These items had lost so much value that the Haussner's never paid more than $3,200 for any painting. They kept to a strict annual budget of $15,000, and Mrs. Haussner was particularly proud that all but two paintings were purchased in the United States. The restaurant's once male-only "stag bar" (open to both sexes in the '70s) was decorated with paintings of tasteful nudes that Mr. Haussner had proudly purchased from art galleries in New York and Atlantic City. With 780 paintings and every bit of wall space occupied, the couple hung their last painting in 1963. In late 1999, following its closing, the finest of the collection was auctioned off at Sotheby's in Manhattan while the remainder was sold at auction in Baltimore. The total was over $11 million. The 1892 painting of a little girl standing with her St. Bernard titled *"I'se Biggest"* brought $673,500, a record for its artist, Arthur John Elsley.

The first item to be auctioned in Baltimore was the 825-pound ball of string which went to Robert Gerber of The Antique Man for $8,250. The creation of this ball began as a clever idea of Mrs. Haussner's to remind her staff not to use the linens for cleaning. The Haussner's daughter, Francie Haussner George, personally rolled much of the twine herself, which came from the strings tied around bundles of laundered napkins. Mrs. George and her husband Stephen George would eventually take over the day-to-day management of the restaurant when Mrs. Haussner reduced her full-time schedule.

Three large bright dining rooms on the main floor could accommodate 500. Tables were always set with white tablecloths, napkins and bread baskets filled with pumpernickel, rye, Kaiser rolls, onion rolls, beaten biscuits and a variety of muffins loaded with chocolate chips, blueberries and poppy seeds. Dark paneled walls were crammed full of paintings. There were portraits, landscapes, and beloved dogs and cats. Every nook-and-cranny was filled with crystal, china, etchings, carvings, porcelains, clocks, bronzes and marble figures. First-time guests experienced a sense of wonderment while taking in what could only be described as a feast for the eyes. I laughed aloud when I read one columnist's initial impression, "It was like being in the storage room of a museum." To put it into perspective, one particular year Haussner's had 1,000,000 visitors see their art compared with the Baltimore Museum of Art's 160,000! Just imagine that.

Haussner's extensive menu was filled with a wide variety of selections from Bavarian German fare, like sauerbraten, schnitzel, spaetzle, hasenpfeffer, and sauerkraut, to traditional Maryland dishes of crab imperial, oysters, Smithfield ham and even Diamondback turtle before it went out of favor. With a menu that included over 112 entrées, everything was prepared to order. The variety appealed to tastes ranging from Champagne to beer. Many Baltimoreans went for the German food. Among these were former Governor and Mayor William Donald Schaefer and his longtime companion, Hilda Mae Snoops. They tried to get there at least once a week, she for the sauerbraten, and he for the fresh vegetable plate, which involved selecting from 35 items, including German potato salad, stewed tomatoes, Tyrolean dumplings, creamed spinach and fried eggplant. Plentiful, reasonable, dependable and unpretentious.

There was even a bakery counter right in the dining room that turned out cakes, pastries and specialty pies. If you hadn't left room for dessert you could take one home with you. At its peak Haussner's staff numbered 210, with 50 in the kitchen. Friendly waitresses, dressed in immaculate white uniforms, many from the neighborhood, bustled between the kitchen and dining room, their service carts loaded with platters. They maneuvered around marble busts of Roman emperors and the occasional coat rack. Many were loyal veterans, some with over 50 years at Haussner's! The restaurant staff could serve 1,500 on a Saturday night and due to sheer volume, the kitchen and waitresses were fast. Haussner's did not accept reservations, so the waiting line usually stretched around the block.

In those final days after the announcement that Haussner's was closing for good, thousands of loyal and curious fans waited in line, sometimes for hours, for one final taste of what would soon be a memory. Patrons left the restaurant with souvenir menus, boxes of baked goods, and some with videotapes of their last meals.

There was a civility to dining at Haussner's - a family place where people came neatly attired to celebrate birthdays, anniversaries, or other occasions. It seemed to be a throwback to happier, simpler times. No music, just the sounds of cheerful chatter and the clatter of silverware. It was not just about the food, the art, or the loyal and hard-working employees showing respect for customers and pride in their product. It was the TOTAL experience. It just made people feel good. Pure and simple. I count my blessings that I was fortunate enough to have witnessed first-hand the unforgettable Haussner's experience; I bet you do too.

Baked Herbed Oysters Haussner's

These baked oysters are so flavorful! The buttery breadcrumb topping adds crunch while the lemon juice brings the right amount of zing.

Serves 7 as a first course

+ **28** fresh shucked oysters, leaving oysters in bottom half of shell
+ **1 cup** of clarified butter
+ **½ cup** fresh minced parsley leaves
+ **3** garlic cloves, mashed to a paste
+ **1 cup** fresh breadcrumbs
+ **½ cup** freshly grated Parmesan cheese
+ **2 teaspoons** paprika
+ Lemon wedges

Preheat oven to 400°F. Arrange the oysters on a bed of rock salt in a baking pan. In a small saucepan, combine melted butter, parsley and garlic. Cook over moderate heat, stirring for two minutes. Let cool.

In a medium bowl, combine fresh breadcrumbs, grated Parmesan and paprika. Divide the butter mixture among the oysters, and top each with the breadcrumb mixture. Bake oysters for 7 minutes or until breadcrumbs turn golden brown. Transfer oysters in their shells to heated plates and serve with lemon wedges.

Tomato Florentine Soup

Nancy Cohen, owner of Eddie's of Roland Park, believes this recipe was served at Haussner's. It came from one of her chefs, who had once worked there.

Makes 4 to 6 servings

+ 1 yellow onion, chopped
+ 2 **tablespoons** olive oil
+ 1 **bag (8 to 10 ounces)** chopped, frozen spinach
+ 1 **48-ounce** can California crushed tomatoes in juice
+ 1 **6-ounce** can tomato paste

+ **6 ounces** Heinz ketchup
+ **1 pint** low-sodium chicken broth
+ Pinch dried basil
+ Pinch of sugar
+ Salt and pepper, to taste

In a heavy bottomed medium stockpot, sauté the chopped onion in olive oil until softened. Add crushed tomatoes, tomato paste, ketchup and chicken broth, bringing it to a boil. Lower heat and simmer 30-45 minutes. Add the frozen spinach, sugar, basil, salt and pepper. Heat through and serve hot.

Grilled Salmon Kebobs

You could broil these, but they are fantastic prepared on a grill too. Longer marinating results in enhanced flavor and moistness.

Serves 4

+ 3 **pounds** fresh salmon steaks
+ 1 medium green pepper
+ 1 medium mild white onion
+ 16 medium-sized fresh mushrooms, cleaned with stems removed
+ 16 firm cherry tomatoes
+ 1 **bottle** creamy Italian salad dressing
+ 8 metal skewers
+ *Seasoned Lemon Rice* (recipe follows)

Remove bones from salmon steaks and cut fillets, with skin on, into 24 pieces. Core green pepper and cut in half. Cut each half into 8 pieces. Repeat with the onion. Begin threading skewers with 3 salmon pieces, 2 onion chunks, 2 green pepper chunks, 2 mushrooms and 2 tomatoes. Repeat procedure with remaining 7 skewers.

Place the completed skewers in a shallow baking pan. Marinate in the Italian dressing for at least 3 hours in the refrigerator. Broil on high heat or grill until fish is cooked through. Serve two kebobs on a bed of seasoned rice.

Seasoned Lemon Rice
Serves 4

+ 1 **cup** long-grain rice
+ 1 **teaspoon** lemon dill herb mix
+ Pinch white pepper
+ Juice from 1 lemon
+ 1 lemon, cut in 8 wedges to garnish

Cook rice according to package directions. Stir in lemon dill herb mix, pepper, and lemon juice. Serve hot.

Hasenpfeffer

Much like the preparation of sauerbraten, hasenpfeffer is a braised rabbit stew in which the meat has first been tenderized by a long soaking in a sour-spiced vinegar marinade. Haussner's served it with spaetzle drenched in butter, to counteract the sourness and, a side of tart red cabbage. Instead of rabbit, this dish can also be prepared using chicken.

Serves 4

+ 1 rabbit, cut in serving pieces
+ 1 **cup** water
+ 1 **cup** vinegar or red wine
+ 1 clove garlic
+ 1 bay leaf
+ 6 peppercorns
+ ¼ **teaspoon** dried thyme

+ ¼ **teaspoon** dried rosemary
+ 1 sliced onion
+ ¼ **cup** butter
+ ¼ **cup** flour
+ ½ **cup** sour cream

In a saucepan, bring water, vinegar, spices and onion to a boil. Reduce heat and simmer for 5 minutes. Cool slightly. Place rabbit in a shallow dish and pour marinade over pieces, cover and refrigerate 24-48 hours, turning occasionally. Remove rabbit from marinade and pat dry with paper towels, reserving the marinade.

Fry in butter until browned. Add flour to skillet stirring until lightly browned. Add one cup of strained marinade and stir to combine. Cover and let simmer gently for 1 ½ hours, or until rabbit is tender, adding more marinade as necessary. Remove rabbit from skillet and stir in sour cream to make a sauce. Serve with spaetzle.

Famous for
FINE FOOD
and
FINE ART

Spaetzle Haussner's

The literal translation for these tiny little German dumplings is "little sparrows." They are easy enough to make using either a flat grater or a spaetzle maker.

+ **2 cups** all-purpose flour
+ **½ teaspoon** salt
+ **¼ teaspoon** freshly grated nutmeg
+ **2** large eggs, beaten lightly
+ **½ cup** milk
+ **¼ cup** chicken broth
+ **3 tablespoons** unsalted butter

In a large bowl, combine flour, salt and nutmeg and stir in beaten eggs. Gradually add milk and chicken broth, beating the mixture with a wooden spoon until it is a smooth soft dough.

Bring 6 quarts of water to a boil in a large pot. Arrange a very coarse grater, smooth side up, over the pot, and with the back of a wooden spoon press dough through the grater. Stir the noodles gently to separate them. Gently boil them for 20 minutes, stirring occasionally. Drain the noodles, transfer them to a bowl of cold water and drain well. In a large nonstick skillet over moderate heat melt the butter and add the noodles to heat through. Transfer to a heated serving dish.

Hungarian Goulash

What better way to warm up on a cold day than with this heirloom dish from Haussner's. A richly seasoned beef stew (or soup), it pairs perfectly with potato dumplings or spaetzle. Scrumptious!

Serves 6

+ **3 pounds** boneless chuck, cut into 3" x 1" x 1/2" pieces
+ **6 cups** water
+ **1 cup** tomato paste
+ **1 cup** chopped onion
+ **¼ cup** Worcestershire sauce
+ **2 tablespoons** caraway seeds
+ **1 tablespoon** sweet Hungarian paprika
+ **1 ½ teaspoons** each salt and pepper
+ **1 ½ teaspoons** fresh thyme or **½ teaspoon** dried
+ **¾ teaspoon** dry mustard
+ **1** large garlic clove, minced
+ **1** bay leaf
+ Parsley for garnish

In a stainless-steel stockpot or enameled Dutch oven combine all ingredients. Bring the liquid to a boil and let simmer gently for 1 hour and 30 minutes or until meat is tender and liquid is thickened. Discard bay leaf. Season with additional salt and pepper to taste. Transfer to a warmed serving dish and sprinkle with chopped parsley. Serve with potato dumplings.

Potato Dumplings Haussner's

Drizzle a little browned butter or gravy over these German dumplings and serve them up as a side dish. I like to serve them with sausage and sautéed red cabbage. Old-world comfort food, plain and simple.

Makes 12 dumplings

For croutons:

Cut slices of day-old bread into ½-inch cubes, making 24 cubes. Melt 2 tablespoons of unsalted butter in a skillet over moderate heat and toss the bread cubes until they are golden brown and crisp. Transfer to a plate lined with paper towels to drain.

+ **2 ½ pounds** unpeeled baking potatoes
+ **2/3 cup** flour
+ 3 large eggs, beaten lightly

+ **1/3 cup** sifted cornstarch
+ Freshly grated nutmeg, to taste
+ Salt and pepper, to taste

Place potatoes in a large saucepan and fill with cold water rising 2 inches above the potatoes. Bring potatoes to a boil and simmer, partially covered, for about 40 minutes, or until tender. Drain the potatoes and in the saucepan, steam them dry, covered, moving the pan for 3 minutes.

When potatoes are warm, but cool enough to handle, peel and puree them through a ricer into a bowl. Add flour, eggs, cornstarch, nutmeg, salt and pepper and beat the mixture until well combined, adding more flour if necessary, to make a soft but not sticky dough. Evenly divide the dough into 12 pieces, rolling each piece around 2 of the croutons to form a ball, and dust with flour. In a stockpot of simmering salted water, poach the dumplings for 15 minutes or until they float to the surface and are firm. To drain, transfer dumplings to a plate lined with paper towels.

Tyrolean Dumplings Haussner's

The next time you fry up some bacon, do not throw the grease out...make dumplings. Tyrolean dumplings, that is. Tyrolean cuisine draws from the mountains and valleys of the Alpine region of Austria. Dumplings prepared with bacon are a popular and important part of that region's cuisine and are usually served in a bowl of flavorful broth or with a hearty portion of sauerkraut.

Makes 20 dumplings

+ **2 pounds** good quality white bread
+ **4 cups** milk
+ **¼ cup** bacon grease
+ **1 tablespoon** Worcestershire sauce
+ **1 tablespoon** salt
+ **1 tablespoon** pepper
+ **½ teaspoon** nutmeg
+ **1 medium-large** onion, chopped
+ **2 stalks** celery, chopped
+ **2 eggs**, beaten
+ **½ cup** cornstarch
+ **1 cup** flour, plus extra for dredging
+ Homemade croutons
+ Pinch of thyme

Dice or crumble the bread into a large bowl. Mix with milk and set aside.

In a separate bowl mix the bacon grease, Worcestershire sauce, seasonings (except thyme), onions and celery together. Combine this mixture and beaten eggs with the bread.

Mix the cornstarch and flour together and add to the bread mixture along with the croutons. Mix well and roll into balls. Coat with more flour. Add thyme to a pot of boiling water. Gently drop dumplings into the water one at a time. Cook for 10 to 15 minutes.

Oysters and Smithfield Ham á la Haussner

Does it get any more Maryland than this??

Serves 4

+ *Sauce* (recipe follows)
+ 48 oysters
+ **1 cup** thin strips of Smithfield ham
+ **2 tablespoons** butter
+ Sliced toast

Prepare sauce and set aside. Pick through oysters and remove any bits of shell. Sauté oysters and ham strips in butter, just until edges begin to curl. Add in the sauce and heat through. Serve on toast slices.

Sauce:

+ **2 tablespoons** butter
+ **2 tablespoons** shortening
+ **½ cup** flour
+ **2 ½ cups** chicken stock
+ **1 teaspoon** salt
+ **½ teaspoon** seasoned salt
+ **¼ teaspoon** white pepper
+ **½ teaspoon** Worcestershire sauce
+ Pinch of Turmeric

In a saucepan melt together the butter and shortening. Blend in flour stirring until smooth and bubbly. Gradually add chicken stock, stirring until smooth. Add in remaining ingredients and bring to a boil. Lower heat and cook stirring constantly until thickened, about 1 to 2 minutes.

Paprika Schnitzel Haussner's

(Veal cutlets with Paprika Sauce)

Paprika schnitzel is another variation of wiener schnitzel but topped with a zesty paprika sauce. Haussner's served it with a side of spaetzle but another option might be Roasted Parsnip Puree (page 148).

Serves 4

+ **Four 6-ounce** veal cutlets, about ½" thick
+ Flour for dredging
+ Salt and pepper
+ **2 tablespoons** clarified butter
+ Watercress for garnish
+ *Sauce* (recipe follows)

Prepare the sauce and set aside, keeping it warm. Season cutlets with salt and pepper. Dust them with flour, and in a skillet sauté them in 2 tablespoons of clarified butter. Cook over moderate heat for 2 to 3 minutes, or until golden brown. Transfer the veal to a heated serving platter. Pour the sauce on top and garnish with watercress. Serve the veal with a side of spaetzle.

Sauce:

+ ½ **cup** minced onion
+ **3 tablespoons** unsalted butter
+ **1 tablespoon** sweet Hungarian paprika
+ **1 cup** chicken stock or broth
+ ½ **cup** heavy cream
+ Salt and pepper

In a saucepan melt 3 tablespoons unsalted butter and cook the onions, stirring until softened. Add paprika and cook stirring for 2 minutes. Stir in chicken stock, bring to a boil, and simmer mixture for 5 minutes. Add heavy cream, bring to a boil, and simmer the mixture for about 10 minutes or until slightly thickened. Season to taste with salt and pepper.

Note: Chicken cutlets can be substituted for the veal, if desired.

Roasted Fresh Ham with Fruit and Herb Stuffing

This stuffed ham showstopper makes a great centerpiece for a holiday dinner. Fresh hams take much longer to cook, but the addition of fruits and herbs elevate the flavor of the ham while cooking.

Serves 25 - 30

+ **12-to-16-pound** fresh ham, boned
+ **1 cup** fresh breadcrumbs
+ **½ cup** fresh chopped parsley
+ **3** cloves garlic, finely chopped
+ **4 teaspoons** whole rosemary, crumbled
+ **2 teaspoons** salt

+ **½ teaspoon** white pepper
+ **8 ounces** dried apricots, chopped
+ **16 ounces** dry packed canned sliced apples, finely chopped
+ **2 tablespoons** corn syrup
+ **2 tablespoons** chopped parsley

Preheat oven to 325°F. Combine breadcrumbs, ½ cup parsley, garlic, rosemary, salt and pepper. Add apricots and apples, mixing well.

Lay open fresh ham like a book and flatten meat surface. Spread fruit mixture evenly over the surface to about one inch from edges. Roll the roast and tie in several places with butcher's twine so you have a neat rolled bundle. Rub the outside of the bundle with salt, pepper and rosemary.

Place in a large shallow roasting pan on rack in a slow oven - 25 minutes per pound. Remove roast from oven, glaze with corn syrup and garnish with chopped parsley. Return to oven for 15 minutes. Remove roast to a warm serving platter and allow to sit in warm place for ½ hour before carving.

Weiner Schnitzel with Anchovies and Capers

Francie Haussner George shared her father's classic breaded veal cutlet recipe with Bon Appétit magazine for their special millennium issue that coincided with the restaurant's 1999 closure.

Serves 6

+ **12** anchovy fillets, coarsely chopped
+ **¼ cup** drained capers, chopped
+ **6** veal cutlets, 3-to-4-ounces each
+ **4** large eggs
+ **1 cup** flour

+ **3 ½ cups** (about) fresh breadcrumbs made from crustless French bread
+ **6 tablespoons (¾ stick)** butter
+ **6 tablespoons** olive oil
+ **3** lemons, cut into wedges

Preheat oven to 200°F. Place anchovies and capers in small bowl; set aside. Between sheets of waxed paper pound cutlets to a ¼-inch thickness. Sprinkle with salt and pepper. Whisk eggs in large bowl. Place flour and breadcrumbs in separate shallow dishes. Dip cutlets into flour, then eggs, then crumbs to coat.

In a large heavy skillet melt 2 tablespoons butter with 2 tablespoons oil over medium-high heat. Add 2 cutlets to skillet; cook until golden brown and cooked through, about 3 minutes. Transfer to baking sheet and keep warm in oven. Using paper towels, wipe skillet clean; repeat with remaining butter, oil and cutlets in 2 more batches. Divide cutlets among plates and sprinkle with anchovy-caper mixture. Serve with lemon wedges.

Fried Eggplant

I must admit that I let out a squeal of delight when I discovered this recipe in a community cookbook (1976) I found as I rummaged through books at a local thrift store. Just when I had given up hope of ever finding it, there it was! Not your ordinary side dish; some loyalists considered it the Holy Grail of Haussner's veggies.

Serves 2

+ 1 small eggplant, unpeeled and sliced ¼-inch thick
+ Flour
+ Salt and pepper
+ 1 large egg beaten lightly
+ **1 to 2 tablespoons** milk
+ **1 cup** fresh breadcrumbs
+ Vegetable oil for deep-frying

Season about 1/3 cup flour with salt and pepper in a small dish. In a second dish, prepare an egg wash by mixing the egg and a little milk. Place the breadcrumbs in a third dish. Dredge each eggplant slice in flour, coating thoroughly and shaking off excess. Coat with the egg wash and dredge in the breadcrumbs, pressing gently to make them adhere. Transfer the eggplant to paper towels to allow them to dry slightly. In a heavy skillet fry the eggplant slices in ½-inch of vegetable oil at 375°F for a minute per side, or until golden brown. Transfer with tongs to paper towels to drain before serving.

Strawberry Soup

Chilled strawberry soup is the ideal refreshment on a hot summer day. You will be amazed that just five ingredients can create something so spectacular.

Serves 4

+ **1 pint** fresh strawberries, hulled; reserve 4 for garnish
+ **2 cups** plain low-fat yogurt
+ **¾ cup** sour cream
+ **¼ cup** honey
+ **1 ounce** strawberry schnapps
+ Sour cream for garnish

Combine all ingredients in a blender and purée until smooth. Refrigerate at least 1 hour before serving. Garnish each bowl with a strawberry and a dollop of sour cream.

Lemon Chiffon Cake

Harry Baker, a California insurance salesman and home baker turned caterer, wanted to improve on the angel food cake that was so popular in the 1920s. He created a lighter and richer recipe in 1927 and is credited with inventing the original chiffon cake. Word spread and Harry was selling his cakes around Los Angeles to Hollywood stars and to the famous Brown Derby Restaurant - remember that hilarious episode of I Love Lucy "Hollywood at Last," when a star-struck Lucy, along with Fred and Ethel encounter William Holden seated in the adjacent booth? Anyway, Harry kept the recipe a secret until 1947 when he sold it to General Mills who published it the following year in Better Homes and Garden magazine. It became a nationwide sensation when the secret ingredient, vegetable oil, was revealed. Incidentally, I also discovered that National Lemon Chiffon Cake Day is observed annually on March 29th.

Makes one 10" tube cake

+ **8** egg whites, at room temperature
+ **1/8 teaspoon** cream of tartar
+ **1 cup + 5 tablespoons** sugar
+ **2 ½ cups** cake flour
+ **1 ¼ teaspoons** baking powder
+ **1/8 teaspoon** salt
+ **1/8 teaspoon** vanilla
+ **1/8 teaspoon** lemon extract
+ **½ cup + 2 tablespoons** egg substitute
+ **¾ cup** water
+ **½ cup** olive oil

Glaze:

+ **1 ¼ cups** sifted confectioners' sugar
+ **2 tablespoons** orange juice
+ **1 teaspoon** lemon juice
+ **1 tablespoon** orange rind, grated
+ **1 teaspoon** lemon rind, grated

Preheat oven to 350°F. Whip the egg whites with a hand-mixer for about 2 minutes. Very slowly, add the cream of tartar and ½ cup + 3 tablespoons sugar, whipping to form stiff peaks. Set aside.

In a separate bowl, mix the cake flour, baking powder, and remaining sugar and salt. Then add vanilla, lemon extract, egg substitute, water and olive oil. Fold in the reserved whipped egg-white mixture.

Bake in an ungreased tube pan for 30 minutes. Allow to cool for 15 to 20 minutes and remove from pan. To prepare the glaze: blend together confectioners' sugar, orange juice, lemon juice, orange and lemon rinds. Drizzle over finished cake.

Maria's "300"

Neighborhood: Little Italy

300 Albemarle Street

Open: 1934 - 1977

How about a little Baltimore history, Italian style? Before World War II, the most famous of Little Italy's restaurants was Maria's "300". It was not the area's first restaurant, but Maria Allori put Baltimore's Little Italy on the culinary map both nationally and locally. Maria's set the standard against which all others would be measured.

The former Maria Cavaliere was born on Exeter Street in 1905. Growing up she lived next door to an Italian woman who spoke no English, but this neighbor was a natural-born cook and Maria would visit her every day and learn her cooking secrets. While still a young girl, Maria waitressed at the Hotel Caswell. By 1923 she had clearly made her mark there. Many of her hotel customers (some influential in the city) inquired about where they could go for real, authentic Italian food. Maria heard this and pursued her dream of establishing her own restaurant. Following a trip to Italy where she learned more about regional Italian dishes, she opened a one-room restaurant on Albemarle Street that seated 50. It was called The Italian Village. Her vision went far beyond the neighborhood. The first thing she did was to send out invitations to all her old customers from the Hotel Caswell. There she had met many visiting public figures. Later she explained her formula for success, "I saw how it worked: good food and famous people and you got it made!"

The restaurant on Albemarle Street became known as Maria's "300". She expanded it over time, until it took up half a block, and seated 500. Lending to the warm and welcoming atmosphere was a professional violinist-around-town and extrovert, Max (Rathje), who serenaded diners at Maria's for 28 years. When was the last time you were entertained over dinner by a strolling, request-taking violinist?

Celebrities were photographed eating bowls of spaghetti with a smiling Maria posing over their shoulders. She always wore her clean white apron, and her long, dyed jet black hair was neatly secured with her trademark single red rose. She used to say, "I brought all the celebrities to Little Italy. That's how Little Italy's restaurants became so popular. I made them famous... Look," she would gesture at pictures spread out before her," here is Max Baer...Ezio Pinza...Jack Carson...Rocky Marciano." She recalled the time when Gene Autry tied up his horse outside on Albemarle Street. Apparently, Autry had been in town to publicize a motion picture.

H. L. "Henry" Mencken made Maria's his location choice for Thanksgiving spaghetti dinner every year. In return, she created Crab Sorrento for him. Al Capone was a "regular" too. In November 1939, following his release from prison, Capone was transported to Union Memorial Hospital where he was being treated for tertiary syphilis. Every night he had dinner brought into his room, and his restaurant of choice was Maria's. Worried about his enemies retaliating, he brought in a food taster to ensure he would not be poisoned. He was a devotee of her Chicken Cacciatore and loved her garlic bread better than any he could get in Chicago. On one occasion, Capone sent his lieutenant, Ralph to the restaurant, where Ralph asked Maria if he might inspect her kitchen. In 1987 her daughter, Louisa Kerber, told Gilbert Sandler of The Evening Sun that her late mother screamed at Ralph, "'Nobody checks up on Maria's cooking. Not even Al Capone. Out!' He got out."

What a character! I would love to have met Maria Allori. She radiated a tireless, joie de vivre philosophy. Maria was as well known for her hospitality as she was for her cooking. She gave back to her community, gifting the Baltimore Zoo with two flamingoes as s part of a new bird exhibit that was opening in 1952.

 For the record, I do not recall ever going to Little Italy as a child, but the neighborhood has always fascinated me. Maybe because my parents never took me there... I do not believe either one of them was over the moon for Italian-American food. By the time I was old enough to drive though, I enjoyed taking my cousins visiting from England down to Little Italy and proudly showing them the area. I took great pleasure in playing tour guide. On other occasions I recruited friends to spend afternoons strolling the neighborhood. We would eventually stop at one of the many restaurants to enjoy a hearty dish of pasta, all the while soaking up the close-knit community spirit that always seems to endure. It was a world apart from the one I'd grown up in Lutherville, yet I could be down there in 20 minutes tops!

With my curiosity piqued, I wanted to learn more about the woman credited with turning Baltimore's Little Italy into a national destination, so I turned to longtime family friend, Pat Thomas, who is well acquainted with just about all of the establishments that I write about. Pat shared with me that her father, Thomas Andre, was raised in Little Italy. His is the first name listed on a plaque at Saint Leo's Church honoring the men from Little Italy who served in World War I. He had enlisted in the navy in April of 1917 and Maria knew him from the neighborhood and simply "adored him." Pat said that she started "going to Maria's as a kid and Maria ran a great restaurant!" When her father occasionally returned to the old neighborhood (he had moved out of Little Italy) with his young family in tow, he and Maria would enjoy conversing in fluent Italian. She took great pleasure in serving them all her specialties, compliments of the house. Now, that's a hostess!

Maria remained at the helm until her retirement in 1971 when she turned over the operation to her granddaughter, Maria Orendorff. Maria Allori died at the age of 68 in 1974. By 1977, the IRS had placed a seizure notice on the front door claiming delinquency of back taxes and shortly thereafter the space was taken over by a new Italian restaurant, Russo's.

1954 advertisement for Maria's "300" restaurant.

Postcard of the Hotel Caswell (1905 – 1927). *Author's collection.* Maria Allori starts her career as a waitress here in 1923 and discovers that the formula for success is "hard work, good food and famous people."

Garlic Bread

I found this recipe on Chowhound quite by accident. Following a comment thread, I came across Joe H., who shared that he became a regular at Maria's in the early '70s. He said that she made the "most incredible garlic bread" that he had ever had. He found out that the waitresses prepared the garlic bread for their customers - not the kitchen. Joe H. "tipped well" and over time learned the recipe and says, "There is NO recipe you will ever find that makes garlic bread as good as this. None." This is his "specialty," the result of thirty years of trying.

+ 1 loaf GOOD, crusty Italian bread cut in ¾" thick slices

+ 1 ½ sticks unsalted butter, softened

+ 1 small to medium bulb of garlic, smashed and minced (yes, lots of cloves)

+ Reggiano Parmigiano cheese, grated

+ Caraway seed (the *secret* ingredient)

+ Chopped fresh basil

+ Hot pepper flakes

Preheat oven to 350°F. Mix fresh garlic and softened butter. Spread enough of the mixture so that you have 1/8-inch thick coating over the entire slice of bread, about 2 tablespoons. Place each slice on a baking sheet. Spread chopped basil over slices. Top with grated cheese to cover completely. Sprinkle 1/8 teaspoon of caraway seeds over each slice. Shake some hot pepper flakes on top. Bake at 350°F for 5 minutes. Serve hot, right out of the oven. Mangia!

Beef Braciola

After "considerable thought and soul searching" Maria Allori decided to reveal her secret recipe for beef braciola to The Evening Sun in 1949.

Serves 4

+ **1 ½ pounds** top round beef, sliced thin
+ 1 clove garlic, chopped finely
+ **¼ pound** prosciutto ham
+ 2 hard-boiled eggs, thin sliced
+ **2 tablespoons** grated Parmesan cheese
+ **1 teaspoon** chopped parsley
+ **1 teaspoon** salt
+ **1 teaspoon** pepper
+ **½ cup** olive oil, divided
+ 1 clove garlic, chopped
+ **2 ½ pounds** canned tomatoes, hand-crushed

Tenderize each piece of top round beef by pounding to about 6 inches in diameter and rub with garlic. Cut the prosciutto to fit on top of beef slices and layer on the hardboiled egg slices. Follow by sprinkling with grated cheese, salt, pepper and parsley. Roll up in jelly roll fashion and secure with toothpicks. Preheat a skillet adding ¼ cup of olive oil and 1 clove of chopped garlic, and braise the rolls turning to brown them evenly. When well browned, add the tomatoes and the remainder of olive oil and simmer for 20 to 30 minutes or until tender. Remove the toothpicks and serve with the tomato sauce. The same sauce can be used with a pound of spaghetti.

Capriccio

Neighborhood: Little Italy

242 South High Street

Open: 1976 - 1996

Baltimore's Little Italy has always been celebrated for its old-school, southern Italian restaurants serving up dishes heaped in red sauce. In the '70s Americans had a growing interest in authentic regional Italian foods, and northern Italian dishes became a fashionable alternative to pasta. Heavily influenced by the French across the border, northern Italian cuisine is generally characterized by its rich and creamy sauces prepared with butter, cream and cheese. In 1976, when partners Rudy Speckamp and Bruno Vigo opened Capriccio on the corner of Fawn and High Streets, it was the first establishment in Little Italy to specialize in northern Italian fare and was altogether unique to Baltimore.

Capriccio (which means "whim" in Italian) was a small neighborhood restaurant that I found very charming. The owners were usually present and could often be found chatting up customers. The main floor dining room was furnished with 14 or 15 small, closely placed tables, the bar and a waiter's station. The décor was somewhat ahead of its time, with its exposed brick walls accented with green velvet draperies, a crystal chandelier and plants, both real and artificial. Tables were set with white and celery napery, attractive wine glasses, and flatware. Attentive waiters in black tie and soft classical background music added to the aura. Even with these formal touches it was still Little Italy and the accent was on casual dress. It became immensely popular with locals and even the occasional celebrity. When Anthony Quinn was in town to play *Zorba the Greek*, he would make the rounds of Little Italy eateries; Capriccio was a favorite on his radar.

Capriccio's signature appetizer was the flavorful Toast Capriccio, a wonderful creation of chef Rudy. Basically, it's a shell created from a hunk of hollowed out Italian bread that has been deep fried, and filled with a mixture of mussels, shrimp, mushrooms, and diced fresh tomato in a creamy dill sauce. Oh my! Veal was at the heart of the menu and prepared in a variety of ways including the house specialty, Veal Capriccio. Other popular choices included oysters Portofino, Scampi Capriccio and an extensive selection of pastas. Dessert offerings included chocolate mousse, Zabaglione with fresh strawberries, cherries jubilee and Italian favorites, cannoli and spumoni.

The partnership eventually ended in 1979 when Speckamp departed. A few years later he would team up with Rudi Paul (longtime maître d' of Peerce's

Plantation), and they would open Rudys' 2900, a premier restaurant in Carroll County. By late 1979, Giovanni Rigato was in place as Capriccio's new owner-chef. Many years later, Rigato would go on to establish the successful Boccaccio Ristorante on Eastern Avenue in Little Italy. In 1981 *Gourmet Magazine* ran a feature article on Baltimore titled *Gourmet Holidays* by Suzanne Patterson. The article highlighted Capriccio among other fine Baltimore restaurants and revealed a series of recipes from some of the city's top chefs. The recipes here are credited to the earlier owner/chefs of Capriccio, Rudy Speckamp and Giovanni Rigato. In 1996, Rocco Gargano, a former waiter at Capriccio, bought the restaurant and renamed it Rocco's Capriccio. He enjoyed a long successful run until it closed in 2013.

Toast Capriccio

This is a signature creation of chef Rudy Speckamp. It's easy to make at home and can be prepared with the addition of any seafood or chicken.

Serves 4

+ **Four** 2 ½" thick slices homemade-type white bread
+ Peanut oil
+ **4 dozen** mussels
+ **4** shallots
+ **2** cloves garlic
+ **1 cup** white wine
+ **1 cup** cream
+ **¼ pound** sliced mushrooms
+ **2 tablespoons** butter
+ Dill
+ Salt
+ White pepper, to taste
+ Juice of ½ a lemon
+ **¼ teaspoon** Worcestershire sauce
+ ROUX (**2 tablespoons** melted butter and **2 tablespoons** flour)

Toast the bread lightly on one side. From the untoasted side, scoop out the crumbs, leaving a thick shell. Brush each shell with 1 tablespoon peanut oil, and toast the bread, oiled side up, on a baking sheet in a 375°F preheated oven for 10 minutes or until golden. Keep the toast warm.

Place butter, shallots and garlic in a casserole dish and cover with mussels. Glaze with white wine. Cover and steam until mussels pop open. Remove from heat. Take mussels out of shells and strain liquid. In a saucepan, add sliced mushrooms and strained liquid and boil for two minutes. Remove from heat and add the cream. Bind with roux. Add dill, salt, white pepper, lemon juice and Worcestershire sauce. Add mussels and heat through. Adjust seasonings if necessary. Place in equal amounts over bread slices. Serve immediately.

Rigatoni alla Vodka

Joanna's Restaurant in New York City made a simple vodka-enhanced pasta dish that started a trend in America in the 1980s. The Capriccio version is so full of flavor thanks to the addition of pork bones and long, slow simmering.

Serves 6 as a first course

+ **½ pound** pork bones, coarsely chopped
+ **1/3 cup** chopped carrot
+ **1/3 cup** chopped onion
+ **1/3 cup** chopped celery
+ 1 large garlic clove, minced
+ **3 tablespoons** olive oil
+ **32-ounce can** Italian plum tomatoes, including the juice
+ **½ cup** tomato purée

+ Cheesecloth bag containing **4** peppercorns and **2** bay leaves, **¼ teaspoon** sugar, salt and pepper to taste
+ **½ cup** cream
+ **1/3 cup** vodka
+ Tabasco
+ **1 pound** rigatoni pasta, cooked al dente
+ **1/3 cup** freshly grated Parmesan cheese

In a large stainless steel or enameled saucepan, over medium heat, cook pork bones, carrot, onion, celery and garlic in olive oil stirring occasionally for 10 minutes or until vegetables are golden. Add the plum tomatoes, juice, purée, cheesecloth bag and bring liquid to a boil. Simmer for 1 hour and 30 minutes, stirring occasionally. Discard pork bones and cheesecloth bag and purée the mixture through a food mill or immersion blender into a bowl. In a stainless steel skillet combine the purée, heavy cream, vodka and Tabasco. Salt and pepper to taste and cook stirring until mixture is heated through. Add rigatoni and Parmesan, tossing the mixture well before transferring to a warmed serving dish.

Scampi Capriccio

(Baked Herbed Shrimp)

Serves 6

+ 1/3 **cup** minced shallots
+ 3 garlic cloves, minced
+ 2 **tablespoons** plus 2 sticks (1 **cup**) unsalted butter, divided
+ ½ **cup** dry white wine
+ 5 **tablespoons** tarragon vinegar
+ 3 **tablespoons** fresh tarragon or 1 **tablespoon** dried
+ ½ **teaspoon** Worcestershire sauce
+ 18 large shrimp, tails intact, deveined and halved lengthwise
+ Fresh minced parsley

Preheat oven to 425°F. In a small saucepan melt 2 tablespoons butter over moderate heat and cook the shallots and garlic, stirring until softened. Add dry white wine, tarragon vinegar, fresh tarragon and Worcestershire sauce cooking over moderately high heat until reduced to about 2 tablespoons. Allow mixture to cool.

In a bowl, cream the remaining butter until softened. Add reduced mixture slowly to butter, whisking vigorously until well combined. Salt and pepper to taste. Divide the shrimp among 6 individual gratin dishes and spread the butter mixture on them. Bake for 7 to 10 minutes, or until the butter is bubbly, and sprinkle with parsley. Serve immediately.

Chicken Gismonda

(Chicken and Spinach with Mushroom Sauce)

Serves 4

+ **Four 8-ounce** boneless chicken breasts
+ Flour
+ 2 large eggs
+ 1 ½ **cups** stale breadcrumbs
+ 1 large garlic clove, minced
+ 1 ½ **tablespoons** olive oil
+ ½ **pound** mushrooms, sliced
+ 1/3 **cup** dry white wine
+ 1 **cup** brown sauce, packaged
+ 1/3 **cup** clarified butter
+ 2 **tablespoons** unsalted butter
+ 1 **pound** spinach
+ Nutmeg

Flatten chicken breasts between two sheets of wax paper with a mallet. Season with salt and pepper and dust them with flour. Beat two eggs in a shallow dish and dip the chicken in the egg allowing the excess to drip off. Coat well with breadcrumbs and chill on a plate for 30 minutes.

In a saucepan, cook the garlic in olive oil over low heat, stirring until softened. Add the mushrooms and cook over moderate heat stirring for two minutes, or until mushrooms are softened. Add the wine, bring to a boil and reduce it by half over high heat. Add the brown sauce and reduce the liquid until slightly thickened. Season sauce with salt and pepper and keep warm.

In a skillet, sauté chicken in clarified butter over moderately high heat for 1 to 2 minutes on each side until golden brown. It can be kept warm in a preheated 200°F oven.

In a large skillet, sauté the spinach in butter over moderate heat for 3 to 5 minutes, or until wilted but still green. Season with nutmeg, salt and pepper.

To serve, arrange the spinach on a heated platter, top with the chicken and drizzle with the sauce.

Veal Scallops with Mozzarella and Prosciutto Capriccio

(Veal Saltimbocca)

Serves 4

+ **1 pound** veal top round cut across the grain into 16 slices
+ **8** paper thin slices prosciutto
+ **4 ounces** thin mozzarella cheese slices
+ **3 tablespoons** olive oil
+ **3 tablespoons** unsalted butter
+ Juice of 1 lemon
+ **1 tablespoon** chopped parsley
+ **1 cup** very dry white wine
+ **¼ cup** chicken broth
+ Flour

Between sheets of wax paper, pound the scallops to a thickness of 1/8 inch. Dust with flour. Sauté the scallops, a few at a time, in olive oil over medium-high heat for about 30 seconds on each side or until browned. Transfer to an ovenproof platter keeping warm.

Drain off the oil and add the white wine, deglazing the skillet. Reduce the white wine by half over moderate heat. Add the chicken broth and reduce by half. Remove the skillet from heat and stir in butter, lemon juice, chopped parsley and salt and pepper. Heat the sauce over low heat, swirling the pan until the butter is melted. Top each scallop with 1 thin slice prosciutto and 1 thin slice of mozzarella, and place under the broiler, about 3 inches from the heat until the cheese is melted. Cover with the sauce and serve hot.

Strawberry Zabaglione

Sweet Marsala is a perfect match for ripe strawberries in this fresh twist on the Italian dessert Zabaglione. It might even be fun to pick your own berries during Maryland's strawberry season which runs from early May through mid-June.

Serves 6

+ 2 large egg yolks, room temperature
+ 1/3 cup sweet Marsala wine
+ 3 tablespoons sugar
+ 1 cup heavy cream
+ 1 tablespoon confectioner's sugar
+ ½ teaspoon vanilla
+ 3 cups strawberries, hulled and halved
+ Amaretti, pulverized (Italian almond macaroons)

In the top of a double boiler placed over simmering water combine egg yolks, Marsala and 3 tablespoons sugar. With an electric mixer beat on high speed until fluffy and tripled in volume. Transfer the mixture to a bowl set in a bowl of ice cubes and stir until the mixture is cold.

In another chilled bowl beat the heavy cream with confectioner's sugar and vanilla until it holds stiff peaks. Fold into the Marsala mixture. Divide the strawberries among 6 Champagne glasses. Spoon the zabaglione over them and finish by sprinkling each with the *amaretti*. Can be refrigerated until ready to serve.

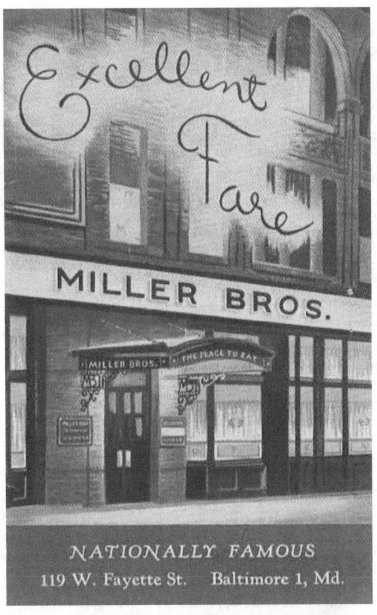

Miller Brothers vintage fold-out postcard, c. 1940's. *Author's collection.*

Miller Brothers Restaurant

"The Place to Eat"

Neighborhood: Charles Center

119 West Fayette Street

Open: 1913 - 1963

For over 50 years, Miller Brothers Restaurant was a premier Baltimore institution known for its fine seafood delicacies and tradition of hospitable service. The crowd that ate there experienced a pervading spirit of warmth, and its time-honored motto of "no music, no frills — the value is on the platter" reflected its pricing. When visitors inquired "Where's a good place to eat in town?" many Baltimoreans mentioned Miller Brothers. One of the most famous restaurants in the United States, it had gained its national reputation for fine food, especially fresh Atlantic seafood. In favorite restaurant polls, Miller Brothers generally ranked among the top five along with Bookbinders (Philadelphia), Locke-Ober (Boston), Antoine's and Arnaud's (New Orleans).

In 1912, founders John H. (d.1958) and his brother, Frederick W. Miller (d.1931), had taken over Schneider's Old German Café, in operation since 1876. It was located on the south side of Fayette Street between Hanover and Liberty Streets, where today the Radisson Hotel Baltimore sits. They renamed the restaurant Miller Brothers and kept up the tradition of old-time, unhurried and gracious service, offering German-American specialties, and other fine foods of Baltimore and the Chesapeake Bay.

Situated on a corner, Miller Brothers occupied a red brick building, described by longtime *Baltimore Sun* reporter, Carleton Jones, as having an "1890s Toulouse-Lautrec look." It was a beauty, with large Victorian windows, some with stained glass panes. The building itself had survived at least two major fires including, miraculously, the Great Fire of 1904.

Miller Brothers first floor was divided into several dining rooms, the kitchen and the Raw Bar, where many a deal was made over a plate of oysters or clams. Civic pride was on full display in the restaurant's dining room known as the East Room. Its ceiling frieze consisted of dark wood panels that were hand-painted by Baltimore artist G.J. Novikoff, with slogans that boasted of Baltimore "firsts." Did you know that "The first umbrella in the United States was raised in Baltimore, Maryland having been imported from India in 1772?" Or that "Baltimore erected the first monument in this country to Christopher Columbus in 1782?" You get the idea — anything invented or manufactured in Baltimore was depicted here.

The West Room was furnished with forty-eight state seals, bubbling drink decorations, chirping canaries, and goldfish bowls that had been built right into the walls. Children found further delight in the doll on display, whose frilly dress was changed daily. Upstairs, on the second floor, were private dining rooms, often utilized by organizations including the Round Table Luncheon Club who met daily. Established at Miller Brothers in 1933, the stag membership included business leaders, Democratic politicians, chief judges from all the city's courts, and the top ranks of the police force. They were still meeting long after the restaurant closed for business thirty years later.

Miller Brothers was family-friendly too. My Aunt Diane shared that as a child during the '50s, she and my grandparents routinely went to Miller's for their big Sunday meal following church services. Upon being warmly greeted by the Maître d' (likely Ted Cook or Bud Clunk), my grandfather would always request a table with his preferred waiter, Ernie. Ernie's usual station was in the West Room on the right-hand side after entering. Diane recalled that Ernie was "real tall" and, she believed, of Greek descent. With a twinkle in her eye Diane described how Ernie would appear at their table, while balancing a big tray on one shoulder, and present her with a humongous Coca-Cola that had been embellished, much to her delight, with about a dozen skewered Maraschino cherries! I can easily imagine her glee. I even felt a sense of excitement when I was able to confirm that, in fact, there had been a waiter at Miller's by the name of Ernest Doukas! The waitstaff (all-male) were polished professionals, this being their chosen occupation. Many spent their entire careers with Miller Brothers. They took absolute pride in their jobs and had respect for the food and the customers that they served. There was a feeling of warm and genuine friendliness; they knew your name and your preferences.

Over the years the restaurant would grow, room by room, eventually seating 450 people on the first floor. Open daily for both lunch and dinner, the selections on the menu were vast and the fare was always fresh and in-season. You could select from crabs, clams, oysters and lobsters having them prepared in any variety of ways. All the seafood platters were served with half a chicken lobster. I discovered that a chicken lobster is a young lobster weighing a pound or less. Diane mentioned that she and my grandfather would often share one with their meal. This was intriguing to me because I can remember during my own childhood when he would occasionally share a lobster with my little sister, Rebecca. My grandfather was very much a man of tradition. Also in demand was Eastern Shore Diamondback terrapin, canvasback duck and Florida green sea turtle. Early on, exotic wild game was available, ranging from elk to black bear to reindeer. These dishes were eventually removed from the menu as diner's tastes evolved. In cold weather it would not have been unusual to observe the carcass of an elk proudly placed on full display right out on Fayette Street before it was butchered on the premises. That sight must have stopped a few in their tracks! A day or two later, guess what showed up on the menu?

To that end, the menus were printed new every morning, never used twice. Its everyday menu cover featured the recognizable red lobster and glass of wine. Other menu covers were designed with holidays and special events in mind too, like the opening of Friendship Airport (1950) and the Bay Bridge (1952) or the Navy-versus-Air Force game (1960). They supplied large envelopes to fit the menus so patrons could address them to friends and leave them for management to mail. Today, a Miller Brothers menu is very much a collector's item.

Contributing to the Miller Brothers success story were two legendary chefs, Paul Pantzer and Samuel Roggio. Pantzer, a native of Austria, was promoted to head chef in 1929. He held a hatred for the Nazis who annexed his homeland. In memory of the collapse of independent Austria in 1938, Pantzer always wore a black chef's toque. He specialized in Maryland seafood but was renowned for his preparation of whale steak and Lobster Esterhazy. He died suddenly in 1950 at the age of 48. Sam Roggio, who trained under chef Pantzer, was promoted and named head chef following Pantzer's death. He would go on to be Miller Brothers last and longest serving chef. Typical fare included Maryland fried chicken, chicken pot pies and sour beef, but the dishes everyone talked about were the crab and lobster Imperials. Roggio said the "secret" to the dish was in the freshly made mayonnaise prepared right there in the kitchen. In a 1987 interview with the Evening Sun, Roggio, referring to the lobster imperial stated, "we took claw meat and body meat and cut it up into chunks, mixed it with mayonnaise, with a little seasoning. And we never served it but that it was bubbling when it went out to the customer."

So many prominent people patronized Miller's. Dignitaries from all over the world and a rash of stars performing at the nearby Ford's Theater visited the place. Presidents Richard M. Nixon (while Vice President) and John F. Kennedy (while still a U.S. Senator) ate there. During racing season, J. Edgar Hoover was a frequent guest always ordering the rockfish. When celebrities stopped in Baltimore — actors, sports figures, you name it — they all came to Miller Brothers. Stars of the day included, in no particular order... Peter Lorre, Basil Rathbone, Boris Karloff, Gloria Swanson, Milton Berle, Glenn Miller, Don Ameche (he loved the Maryland fried chicken), The Dorsey Brothers, Bette Davis, Katherine Cornell, Clark Gable, Mae West, Walter Huston, and sports figures Jack Dempsey, Ty Cobb, Max Baer, and Babe Ruth. Baltimore resident and outspoken newspaper pundit, H.L. Mencken was a regular.

Sunday, June 30th, 1963, the last day, was a day of reminiscing and melancholy for both waiters and scores of old-time patrons of Miller Brothers, a Baltimore institution for more than half a century. Baltimore had plans to make way for urban renewal, forcing Miller Brothers, and many other nearby businesses to close their doors. The entire city block fell victim to the wrecking ball making way for the redevelopment of Charles Center. The restaurant was revived in 1967 in what was then, the newly built Baltimore Hilton, but to Miller traditionalists, it was light years away from having the original restaurant's appeal. In June of 1963, the *Daily Times* of Salisbury, Maryland ran an opinion piece that ended with "Perhaps we should remember Miller Brothers as we do now, an epicurean treat, the climax to a visit to the city, something akin to the historic Rennert Hotel, gone but not forgotten." There you have it.

Noteworthy: In 1939, John Henry Miller invented and patented the modern-day table Crumber. Less conspicuous than a brush, it could be discreetly carried in a waiter's pocket.

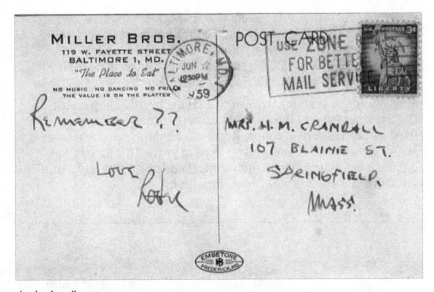

Author's collection

Southern Fried Chicken a la Maryland

In 1942, a Parade Magazine photographer was dispatched to Miller Brothers Restaurant. His objective was to capture the chef's step-by-step preparation of Southern fried chicken in a series of images. The instructions given did not include any measures, so I include it here mostly for historical value. The article went on to say that Miller's served the dish on fresh toast with French-fried potatoes, watercress, and asparagus.

Serves 4

Quarter a chicken. Dredge each piece in flour completely. Prepare an egg wash with a beaten egg and a tablespoon of water and dip the chicken to coat. Next, dip the chicken in a shallow pan of breadcrumbs. In a skillet, fry the chicken in butter on both sides until cooked through. Serve hot or cold.

Note: My editor prepared this simple recipe by including a little Old Bay seasoning to the flour. He shared, "I've tried to make fried chicken before. A couple times I did it right, but I've usually screwed it up, and I haven't even tried in years. This time it was great! Moist, lots of flavor, and though I added the Old Bay, I think it would've been pretty good even without it."

Following the repeal of prohibition, Miller Brothers becomes home to the Round Table Luncheon Club. A 1958 membership card hints that the thin-skinned need not apply.

Crab Imperial

The Action Line was a public service column that ran in U.S. newspapers during the '60s and '70s. Edward Koob of Atlantic City had dined at Miller Brothers and wanted the recipe for what he described as "out of this world" Crab Imperial. Action Line put in the request and sure enough, chef Sam Roggio was happy to accommodate and revealed the special recipe to readers everywhere. He suggested substituting lobster claw and chunks of body meat for the crab if you prefer Lobster Imperial. The secret was in the mayonnaise, made in Miller Brothers kitchen.

Serves 6

+ **8 tablespoons** homemade mayonnaise (page 114)
+ **2** egg yolks, divided use
+ **1 teaspoon** salt
+ **½ teaspoon** white pepper
+ **½ teaspoon** Accent
+ Paprika
+ Juice of 1 lemon
+ **2 pounds** crabmeat, backfin lump only

Preheat oven to 400°F. In a large bowl, mix mayonnaise, egg yolk, salt, white pepper, Accent and lemon juice. Blend the crabmeat with the mayonnaise mixture, being careful not to break up the lumps. Place in prepared individual shells. Brush the tops with a wash made from the other egg yolk and about one tablespoon of water. Sprinkle with paprika and bake for 10-12 minutes until hot and bubbly.

Seafood Lord Calvert

These are like little surprise packages and make such a nice presentation. Chef Roggio liked to prepare this dish at home.

Makes 8 Lord Calvert's

+ **4** filets of sole, about ½ **pound**
+ **¼ cup** finely diced cooked shrimp
+ **¼ cup** finely diced cooked lobster
+ **½ pound** American cheese, sliced into eight 4" squares

Sauce:

+ **1 ½ tablespoons** butter
+ **1 ½ tablespoons** all-purpose flour
+ **1 cup** fish stock
+ **½ teaspoon** salt
+ **½ teaspoon** chopped chives
+ **½ teaspoon** chopped parsley
+ **½ cup** Sauterne wine

Preheat oven to 325°F. Cut each filet in half lengthwise. Form into eight rings and secure with toothpicks. Arrange in a baking dish. Fill the center of each ring with diced shrimp and lobster. Top off each ring with a slice of cheese. Bake in oven for 20 minutes.

For the sauce:

Prepare a roux by melting butter and adding flour to blend. Stirring constantly, add fish stock a little at a time, cooking over low heat until smooth and thickened. Add salt, chives and parsley. Stir in the wine and continue cooking another minute or two. Serve hot over the Lord Calvert's.

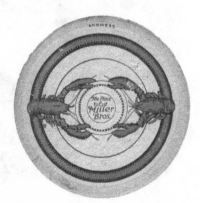

House of Welsh

"Baltimore's Oldest Restaurant Since 1900"

Neighborhood: Downtown Baltimore

301 Guilford Avenue

Open: **1900 – 1998**

The historic House of Welsh embodied a comfortable old-time Baltimore steakhouse. First established as a saloon in 1838 it was considered the oldest continuously operated saloon in the city. Food service started in 1900 and the House of Welsh, as it later became known (it was called The Black Bottle then), was run by three generations of the Welsh family until it closed nearly a century later. The three-story building comprised three 1830s row houses on the corner of Guilford Avenue and Saratoga Street not far from City Hall. During the Great Baltimore Fire of 1904, the House of Welsh played an important role in the city's history. Fire engulfed much of the downtown area. As it approached the main Western Union offices, Associated Press reporters and telegraphers were forced to take to the streets with their equipment and retreat further north. The House of Welsh became the Western Union outpost. Operating from its 3rd floor, telegraphers were able to connect their instruments to the main telegraph lines and fire off reporters' accounts to the rest of the world by Morse Code.

During the '40s the brick building was painted black, with its façade covered in signage that advertised its steaks, chops, private label "Black Bottle" Maryland rye whiskey, ("one sip will bathe the drooping spirits in delight") and National Bohemian beer. The Guilford Avenue Elevated streetcar line (the "El" for short), ran right overhead. The No. 8 streetcar made the aerial trip along the El and came down to the ground at Guilford and Saratoga by The Black Bottle but, the El was demolished in 1950 to make way for transit buses. At some point the premises were enhanced with an application of Baltimore's nostalgic Formstone. Once inside, you felt like you stepped into a time warp. The décor epitomized a distinctly old-fashioned Baltimore row house with its three low-ceilinged dining rooms, knotty pine walls lined with photos of old Baltimore, and Tiffany lamps. The upstairs dining room featured an original 1838 slate fireplace.

The House of Welsh was famous for its big sizzling steaks prepared the "old-fashioned way" and delivered to tables on hot metal trays straight off the broiler. They ran advertisements suggesting it was less expensive to dine at the House of Welsh than at home! In a letter that I received from my friend, Haswell Franklin, Sr., he fondly remembered the House of Welsh, "home of the $1.25 T-bone and the best roll of any restaurant I have ever known."

Those cloverleaf rolls must have been something because the "House of Welsh Special" was a dessert made from a split roll topped with cherry pie filling, ice cream and whipped cream! While noted for its variety of regular and king-sized steaks, the restaurant was also lauded for its seafood dishes.

Although a little off the main drag, it attracted politicians, lawyers, judges, bookmakers, lobbyists, policemen and reporters. They could enjoy plain, good food at a leisurely pace, and deals were made over 30-cent mugs of beer or 40-cent martinis and Manhattans. The bar was males-only and whites-only until the '60s when a federal judge in New York ruled the practice unlawful. In the '90s its bar was a set for the television series, *Homicide: Life on the Street*.

The House of Welsh was sold in 1999 and transformed into an upscale nightclub called Club One. The building was demolished in 2011.

Steaks "the old-fashioned House of Welsh way"

Cooking time required to broil steaks depends on:

1. the quality and uniform thickness of the cut and the extent of the surface area - larger steaks require just a bit longer;
2. the degree of doneness desired;
3. the distance from the source of heat.

Generally, steaks of 1 ½ to 2 inches in thickness should be broiled at 3 inches from the source of heat, while steaks of 1 inch or less should be 2 inches from heat.

There are two schools of thought as to the proper time to season: before or after broiling. In general, it is best to season lightly before and again to personal tastes after broiling.

Steak Seasoning

Before broiling (choose one):

a. rub with mixture of olive oil and a dash of dry mustard
b. brush the steak with crushed garlic or garlic-butter mix
c. brush with melted butter and herbs (oregano, marjoram, and/or rosemary)

After broiling (choose one):

a. dust lightly with salt and pepper
b. finish with bits of butter, sautéed mushrooms, capers, etc
c. spread lightly with prepared mustard.

At the table: Have steak sauces at the ready for those who cannot do without.

Harvey House Restaurant

Neighborhood: Mount Vernon

920 North Charles Street

Open: 1952 - 1993

For over 40 years the Harvey House restaurant and bar was a favorite Baltimore institution located on Charles Street's Restaurant Row in Mount Vernon. Owned by the Baumel family and just steps away from the Washington Monument it was a landmark easily identified by a purple neon tuxedo-clad rabbit named "Harvey" that hung over its door. It has been said that the name was inspired by the Broadway show featuring a famous invisible rabbit, but Harvey was also the given name of the Baumels' son. Before its 1952 opening, Lou Baumel had been a partner in the old Club Charles from 1941-1951, a supper club that had been a popular night club venue featuring relatively unknown entertainers like Jerry Lewis, Dean Martin, Lenny Bruce and singer Tony Bennett. The club had been a popular meeting place until television came along and people began to stay at home and watch entertainment on their new sets. Lou Baumel knew a thing or two about what it took to be successful in the restaurant business, and along with his wife, Rose, they built the reputation of the Harvey House by delivering consistent quality and impeccable service. They catered to all tastes - ranging from "good ol' home style" to exquisite continental cuisine. Avoiding anything terribly fancy, they offered hearty, honest, mostly American food served in a comfortable, homey dining room.

The Baumels understood the importance of growing and maintaining a local Baltimore clientele (as opposed to one-time tourists), and their restaurant became a preferred choice for lunch, dinner and after-theater dining. During its heyday, it was almost club-like, in that everyone seemed to know one another. The crowd had lots in common including attendance at Colt games and Pops performances with the Baltimore Symphony Orchestra. Following a Friday night performance with the BSO in 1991, Tony Bennett even dropped by the Harvey House to chat with Lou about the good old days as a young club crooner. It was an atmosphere of fun, often noisy and crowded, with lots of table-hopping of the likes that one does not generally see much of these days.

Lou enjoyed playing host and being out front by the door to greet his regulars while Rose supervised the kitchen staff and oversaw the office. She was also credited with creating a "home away from home" feeling by furnishing the restaurant with her own personal knick-knacks and antique mahogany curio cabinets filled with sparkling Waterford crystal and floral patterned china of roses and peonies. In later years, there was even a memorial celebrating Elvis.

The dining room was large and always maintained a '50s vibe with waitresses in tuxedo-style uniforms greeting their patrons and taking orders. Many regulars did not even need to see a menu and were so familiar that the staff acknowledged them by name. First up was the relish tray of carrots and celery followed by chopped chicken liver canapés compliments of the house. My friend, Pat Thomas, shared with me that she "loved the Harvey House...it was a happy place with great food and wonderful service. Their chopped chicken livers were the best!" Sauces and stocks were all homemade and meats and vegetables were fresh, never frozen. Single entrées were abundant, and often were enough to serve two.

By all accounts, the lively piano bar was a favorite hangout frequented by the over-45 crowd, who enjoyed their Old-fashioneds and extra-extra dry martinis. An early 1953 advertisement promoted Shad the bartender's original "Flying Saucer" cocktail (apricot brandy, rum, Cointreau, and lemon juice). After one, you are one! On the weekends, the talented Mary True played "cocktail" melodies from the '40s and '50s on the grand piano and sing-a-longs were prevalent and crowd-pleasing. What great fun!

Postcard view of the dining room at the Harvey House, c. 1960s. *Author's collection.*

Borscht

Borscht or beet soup is customarily served with a dollop of sour cream. The Harvey House presented their Borscht in a large, long-stemmed goblet and garnished it with potato wedges.

Serves 4

+ 4 large beets, washed
+ 2 onions, chopped
+ 1 **quart** water
+ 1 **teaspoon** salt

+ 1 **teaspoon** sugar
+ ¼ **cup** fresh lemon juice
+ ½ **cup** sour cream

Peel beets and chop finely. Place in a large saucepan with onion and water. Bring to a boil, reducing heat to a slow simmer. Cover and cook about 35 minutes or until the beets are tender. Puree the soup in the pot with an immersion blender until smooth (or in a stand blender, in two batches). Add salt, sugar and lemon juice. Serve hot or chilled with a dollop of sour cream.

French Onion Soup

After returning from a trip to France, the Baumels began serving this onion soup at the Harvey House. For many years it was one of the most popular items on the menu.

Serves 6

+ 2 large onions, thinly sliced
+ 2 **tablespoons** vegetable oil
+ **6-7 cups** water
+ 1 beef bone
+ 2 **tablespoons** dry sherry

+ French bread sliced and sprinkled with Parmesan cheese and lightly toasted
+ **12** thin slices mozzarella cheese

Preheat oven to 375°F. Sauté the onions over low heat until they begin to take on color. They should be half done at this point. Transfer the onions to a large pot and add water, beef bone, salt and pepper to taste, and sherry. Simmer the stock for 45 minutes to one hour. Ladle the stock into individual ovenproof bowls and place one slice of toasted bread on top of each bowl. Cover each bowl with 2 slices mozzarella.

Place bowls on a baking sheet and into the oven for about 30 minutes or until the cheese is melted and crusty. Serve hot.

Calves' Liver with Bacon

A classic combination of pan sautéed liver and bacon finished in the oven.

Serves 6

+ **2 pounds** calves' liver, ½" thick, skinned and gristle cut away
+ **12** slices good quality bacon

+ Flour
+ Butter

Preheat oven to 325°F. Dredge the pieces of liver in flour, shaking off excess. Sauté in hot butter for 2-3 minutes per side or until half done. Set aside. Meanwhile, gently cook the bacon until half done. Place liver in a casserole dish and cover with bacon slices. Place in oven and cook about 10 minutes.

Homemade Rice Pudding

Top with whipped cream, berries, bananas, chopped nuts—whatever your heart desires.

Serves 6

+ **2 cups** long grain white rice
+ **4 cups** hot water
+ **2 cups** table cream
+ **½ cup** sugar

+ **2 teaspoons** vanilla extract
+ **¼ teaspoon** salt
+ **1 teaspoon** nutmeg
+ **1 teaspoon** cinnamon

In a large saucepan bring rice and water to a boil. Drain and place rice back in saucepan. To the rice, add cream, sugar, vanilla and salt. Cook slowly over low heat, stirring occasionally until the rice "tightens," about 30 minutes. Transfer to individual serving bowls and sprinkle tops with nutmeg and cinnamon. Allow to cool for 20 minutes and serve.

Vintage linen postcard portrays exterior view of Jimmy Wu's New China Inn. *Author's collection.*

Jimmy Wu's New China Inn

Neighborhood: Charles Village

2426 North Charles Street

Open: 1944 - 1983

The popular New China Inn was the most famous Chinese restaurant in Baltimore for nearly 40 years, but the landmark was always referred to as Jimmy Wu's after its legendary owner. A leader in the Chinese community, James L. F. Wu introduced legions of Baltimoreans to Chinese food, Cantonese style. He became a partner in the restaurant when it was on Park Avenue and in 1946 moved it farther uptown to Charles Street just below 25th Street, where it remained a fixture for over 38 years.

The nine-room restaurant, painted in green and brilliant red, was spread out over several row houses, offering several floors with a variety of dining rooms, some accessible by little staircases, and some rooms more formal than others. It was a happy Chinese atmosphere with lanterns and dragons and nameplates hung over the doors that identified the "Confucius Room," "Longevity Room," "Ming Room" and "Forbidden Quarters." It was clean and bright with soft lighting and spotless tablecloths - customers could dress up without feeling out of place.

The cuisine, pure Cantonese, was somewhat modified to suit American tastes with dishes like Egg Foo Young, Chicken Chow Mein and Chop Suey, all served with knives and forks. Diners saw the value in the Famous Family dinners that came with a choice of Won Ton or Egg Drop soup, rice, tea and dessert all for about $6 per person in the '70s. With numerous Chinese options, there was also a complete American menu available, with steak, crab imperial, pot roast, ham steak and pineapple, breaded veal cutlet and chicken a la King.

I recently had lunch at Tark's with my friend, Carol. As a child, Carol and her family often frequented Jimmy Wu's. A kid in a candy store, she loved to linger at the welcoming case full of tchotchkes located near the entrance. She recalled that her family always occupied the same room, one of the smaller dining rooms upstairs. She was convinced it was their own private room and any pesky "party crashers" may have been the unwitting recipients of little Carol's pouty face! Jimmy Wu's was extremely popular with families because there was something for everyone, even if you were not a fan of Chinese food. Case in point, Carol mentioned that her grandfather never varied from ordering his favorite pot roast. She not only has cherished memories of her family's regular gatherings at the restaurant, but she also fondly remembers the warm and hospitable interactions they all had with Mr. and Mrs. Wu.

Service was prompt and friendly and Mr. Wu, known for his warm smile, would visit each table making sure his guests were enjoying a positive dining experience, often taking delight in sharing stories and sometimes, family photographs. Well-versed in marketing, he advertised catchy exotic cocktails like the *Umbra-Lilly*, prepared by his bartender, "Won Long Pour" - "*a hot number! To shade you there's an umbrella speared with maraschino.*"

It became a late-night destination for politicians, ad executives, members of the press and media and professional athletes including Baltimore Colts Artie Donovan, Lenny Moore and Coach Don Shula, who found it a comfortable place to unwind. And, I would be remiss if I left out Orioles players like Brooks Robinson and Jim Palmer.

The New China Inn never really changed. Jimmy Wu stuck with the same winning formula, but with the growth of Chinese restaurants, more and more were riding the Szechuan wave that had taken Baltimore by storm. Jimmy Wu was resistant to the trend, but eventually hired a Szechuan chef - perhaps too late. Either way, by 1983 he sold the restaurant to a Washington restaurateur who immediately renamed it the Szechuan Gourmet.

Less than a year after his retirement, Wu died at the age of 76. Near the end of his life he told the *Baltimore Sun*, "Whether you call it a success or not, life has been rewarding, has been interesting to me. And Baltimore, particularly, has been good to me. And I hope in a way of serving people, introducing them to Chinese food and helping to make Chinese food in the city of Baltimore." He went on to say he felt rewarded by making people happy. Not only did he make people happy, he grew the overall popularity of Chinese food in Baltimore, spurring a host of new restaurants that seemed to pop up almost overnight. Jimmy Wu will be remembered for enriching the lives of so many by sharing with us his culture, traditions and history.

Vintage linen postcard portrays exterior view of Jimmy Wu's New China Inn. *Author's collection.*

Chicken Egg Drop Soup

To usher in the 1966 Chinese New Year, Jimmy Wu and his chef demonstrated this and the following dishes for an international cooking class that was held at the Y.W.C.A., International Center-East Baltimore branch. He adapted these recipes for home use.

Serves 4

+ **1 egg**, beaten
+ **6 cups** chicken broth
+ **½ teaspoon** each, salt and pepper, or to taste

+ **¼ teaspoon** MSG (optional)
+ **1 ½ teaspoons** corn starch

In a large saucepan, bring chicken broth to a boil. Add salt, pepper, and (if using) MSG. Reduce the heat to low. Mix cornstarch into ¼ cup of cold water. Slowly, pour the mixture into the broth stirring constantly as it thickens slightly. Continue stirring while adding the beaten egg. Serve hot.

Carol Townsend (second from right) and family share a light moment in front of Jimmy Wu's on North Charles Street. From left: grandmother Gertrude, grandfather John, sister Karen and cousin Brian, c. March 1971. *Courtesy of Carol T. Jones.*

Butterfly Shrimp

Serves 2

+ **1 pound** fresh jumbo shrimp, shelled
+ **5** slices of bacon
+ **2** eggs, beaten
+ **½** large yellow onion, sliced
+ **1** scallion, sliced
+ **2 tablespoons** tomato sauce
+ **1 tablespoon** Worcestershire sauce

+ **4** dashes Tabasco sauce
+ **¼ teaspoon** MSG, optional
+ **2 cups** chicken broth or water
+ **6** toasted almonds, cracked
+ **1 teaspoon** of cornstarch, dissolved in **¼ cup** cold water
+ **2 tablespoons** corn or peanut oil

Split back of shrimp, but do not cut all the way through. Spread the shrimp out to flatten on a cutting board and remove the vein. Rinse and dry the shrimp with paper towels. Cut each bacon slice into 3 pieces to match the length of shrimp. Gently press them onto the shrimp.

Warm a skillet over moderate heat and add peanut oil. Dip shrimp individually into beaten eggs and place in skillet bacon side down. When bacon becomes crisp, turn shrimp over and cook until done, another 30 to 60 seconds. Remove shrimp from skillet.

Add yellow onions to the skillet and sauté for a couple of minutes. Stir in seasonings and broth. Simmer for 3 minutes covered. Thicken with cornstarch and pour the gravy over shrimp. Serve garnished with chopped scallions and almonds.

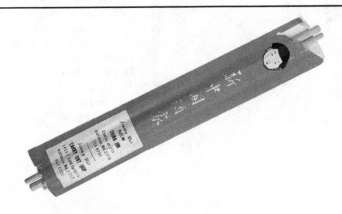

Beef Stir Fry with Tomato

Serves 4

+ 1 ½ **pounds** tender beef (top sirloin or flank steak), cut 1/8" thick slices **(size 1"x 2")**

+ 8 tomatoes, each cut into 6 or 8 pieces

+ ½ **cup** beef stock or water

+ 3 **tablespoons** corn or peanut oil

+ 1 clove garlic, crushed

+ 1 **teaspoon** fresh ginger, sliced or ¼ **teaspoon** of ground ginger

+ Salt and pepper, to taste

+ 1 **teaspoon** sherry wine

+ 2 **tablespoons** cornstarch

+ 2 **tablespoons** soy sauce

+ 1 **teaspoon** sugar

+ ¼ **teaspoon** MSG, optional

In ¼ cup of cold water dissolve cornstarch together with soy sauce, sugar (and MSG, if using). Set aside. Put oil in a hot skillet, add salt, pepper, garlic and ginger. Add beef and wine stirring for 2 minutes; then add tomatoes, stock and cornstarch mixture. Continue to stir carefully for 2 to 3 more minutes until it reaches a boil and is smooth and thickened. Serve with cooked long grain rice.

Carol (second from left) celebrates her brother John "John-John's" (not pictured) first birthday in the Confucius Room. The mirrored back wall makes the private room appear larger and reflects the family, from left: cousin Brian, father Mel, and cousin Steve, c. March 1971. *Courtesy of Carol T. Jones.*

Thompson's Sea Girt House

Neighborhood: Govans

5919 York Road

Open: 1885 - 1991

From my perspective, 1979 was a year of milestones. That spring my best friend Meg and I both graduated from Towson Senior High and we soon found ourselves coming of age. It did not take us long to figure out where the popular watering hole hangouts were in our area, and Jerry's Belvedere Tavern near Northern Parkway certainly fit the bill. The neighborhood bar in Govans was comfortable, friendly and cheap, and we could always rely on catching up with a group of our friends there. It fast became our regular stomping ground. It was from frequenting Jerry's that I actually discovered Thompson's Sea Girt House right across the street.

I had often seen the large overhead signage announcing its presence, but otherwise I was unfamiliar with the place. One evening at Jerry's I found myself in conversation with a couple of fellows who worked as waiters at Tio Pepe's restaurant. Vaguely, I recall that they had some sort of association with Thompson's, perhaps with the chef or someone who worked there in the kitchen.

I should note here that in 1983 the Thompson family sold the Sea Girt House to Tomas Sanz and Jose Sanza. These men had made names for themselves as chef and waiter respectively while at Tio Pepe restaurant. Joining them as a buyer was Bruno Vigo, a former partner in Capriccio. Maybe Tomas and Jose were the gentlemen to whom I was speaking, but I guess that will remain a mystery.

One of these men explained to me that Thompson's was widely known for its popular surf-and-turf-style dinners, especially traditional Maryland seafood specialties, and he strongly recommended the crab cakes. This seemed like an ideal plan to Meg and me... we could enjoy a crab cake dinner before scooting right across the street to spend an evening at Jerry's Belvedere. Perfect! We soon discovered that those classic lump crab cakes were winners; pure and simple. The Thompson's philosophy was to let the sweet crab meat speak for itself, so spices were kept to a minimum and they used just enough binder for the crab cakes to hold their form. Not enormous by today's standards, they were more medium-sized, and fried to a golden brown — less demand then for broiled, which didn't catch on until the late '70s. Little did either of us realize that the delicious crab cake recipe we enjoyed was once the subject of a controversial U.S. Senate debate!

The *Evening Sun* headline of January 26, 1963 read, "Crab Cake Controversy Rages Among Connoisseurs, Chefs." A week earlier, returning from the Senate dining room, Maryland Senator J. Glenn Beall, denounced on the Senate floor, what the Senate dining room was pleased to call Maryland Crab Cakes. Beall declared, "I resent the crab cakes being served in the Senate dining room today being called 'Maryland Crab Cakes.' No Marylander would recognize what was being served. I do not say the crab cakes served are bad. I simply say they fall short of the high standard of Maryland crab cakes, that tasty dish which has helped to make the name Maryland loved throughout the nation."

Then-Governor Tawes' wife, Helen Avalynne Tawes, a native of Crisfield, wrote to Beall over that weekend. In 1958, she had written a booklet called *My Favorite Maryland Recipes* which had been distributed in support of her husband's gubernatorial run. A well-regarded cook, she suggested he pass her "real Maryland seafood" recipes along to the Senate chef. Mrs. Tawes' crab cake recipe was published in the *Congressional Record* followed by newspapers across the country. The story blew up! One headline read *Crab Fest: Avalynne's Recipe Raises the Devil*.

Her version called for a pound of claw meat and included horseradish mustard, a dash of Tabasco sauce and a tablespoon of chopped parsley. Her crab cake recipe was not without its detractors even in the Old Line State. One such detractor was restaurateur George W. Thompson, whose great-grandfather had founded Thompson's Sea Girt House in 1885 when it was situated on the edge of the Chesapeake Bay in lower Canton. Thompson, who used between 800 and 1,000 pounds of backfin crab a week and considered crab cakes to be his specialty, asked, "Whoever heard of one tablespoon of chopped parsley for a pound of meat? I use a tablespoon for 10 pounds of meat. And Tabasco sauce in crab cakes? Never heard of it." Thompson wanted the Senate to taste "real" Maryland crab cakes and offered to prepare a "load" of backfin crab cakes and fry them up in the Senate kitchen. And that he did. The kitchen was mobbed with a bedlam of press photographers and reporters covering the event. Every Senator was invited to the feast for a "taste vote" and they ate nearly 400 crab cakes and almost 10 pounds of coleslaw and potato salad. Approval was unanimous. Then-Vice President Lyndon B. Johnson called Beall's office later and was quoted as saying, "Tell Senator Beall those are the best crab cakes I ever ate, and I want him to have them served once a week until my term runs out." It was not to be though. The chef's hands were tied by budgetary constraints (set by the Senate) and an "authentic" recipe could not be adopted. When the same platter was reinstated on the menu the cost was still $1.05 but they were simply called "fried fresh crab cakes" with no mention of the state of Maryland. Soon afterwards, however, Thompson began a brisk mail order crab cake business.

By the time I began frequenting the Sea-Girt House it was in the hands of a fourth-generation Thompson, George W. "Tommy," and his mother

Margaret. More than once I overheard someone ask, "What's a sea-girt?" For over sixty years, the original restaurant had been located on the lower Canton waterfront on property surrounded by harbor water, hence the name. Often when patrons entered the reception area, Mrs. Thompson was on hand to warmly greet them. Backlit portholes, nautical netting and a tank full of lobsters accented an otherwise traditional décor. The long, narrow, dark paneled main dining room was dimly lit, and divided into two sections by a long and narrow bar running down its center. Comfy and spacious black banquettes for four ran down one side of the room while banquettes for two ran down the other. Fresh red roses were placed on every table. A third dining room at the south end of the restaurant provided tables and chairs only. At the head of the dining room adjacent to the bar was a grand piano and during dinner gentle piano stylings served as background. As the hours passed the pianist might entertain a small group gathered around the piano with sing-along melodies.

The menu emphasized seafood and other house specialties like crab imperial, shrimp scampi, roast prime rib, shad, stuffed rockfish and, of course, crab cakes. The vegetable offerings included stewed tomatoes and delicate thin slices of fried eggplant, said to be favorites of Mrs. Thompson right along with their signature crab cakes. Incidentally, according to *The Encyclopedia of American Food and Drink* by John F. Mariani, Thompson's Sea Girt House was the originator of crab imperial (page 157) sometime during the late 19th century.

Thompson's was simply old-fashioned Baltimore, genuine and comfortable. Over the years it saw the likes of visiting singers and celebrities such as John Denver, Liberace, Johnny Cash, Frank Sinatra and was also well-liked by various Orioles and Colts. Whitey Herzog enjoyed his Thompson's crab cakes at home in St. Louis by FedEx delivery. Unpretentious, it regularly attracted families and more mature couples who simply appreciated the reliable pleasure of predictability.

Meg Schwartzman (right) helps me cut into my birthday cake on June 13, 1983. We've been best friends since tenth grade.

Thompson's Crab Cakes

Here is the signature recipe for Thompson's classic Maryland crab cakes as prepared and served to the United States senators in 1963, courtesy of Thompson's restaurant.

Makes 6 to 8 crab cakes

+ **1 pound** backfin crabmeat
+ **1 ½ tablespoons** finely crumbled cracker crumbs
+ Pinch chopped parsley
+ **2 tablespoons** mayonnaise

+ Dry mustard, to taste
+ **1 egg yolk**, not the whole egg
+ Salt and white pepper, to taste
+ Butter for frying

Place the backfin crabmeat in a large bowl. Sprinkle the cracker crumbs and parsley on top and lightly toss by hand. In another small bowl, combine salt, white pepper, mayonnaise, dry mustard, and egg yolk. Beat together and pour over the crab mixing by hand to prevent breaking up the lumps. Form into 6-to-8 cakes. At this point they can be refrigerated for about an hour. Pan fry in melted butter until golden brown, about 4 minutes per side. Serve with sides of potato salad and coleslaw.

IDlewood 5-1800

ULTIMATE IN SEA FOOD

Thompson's
SEA GIRT HOUSE

Thompson's Crab Fluffs

When a nearby eatery (remember The Yorkshire?) stopped making crab fluffs, Thompson's chef Daniel Pacini formulated this version for the restaurant. Simply put, they are crab cakes dipped in batter. Serve these delectable morsels up with sides of tartar sauce, cocktail sauce and a lemon wedge or two.

Makes 8 fluffs

+ Prepare a pound of crabmeat as for crab cakes. Shape into 8 balls.

+ Vegetable oil for frying

Batter:

+ **2 cups** flour

+ **2 cups** water

+ **2** eggs

+ Salt and pepper, to taste

+ **6 ounces (1 ½ sticks)** butter, softened

Mix batter ingredients to a smooth consistency. Dip crab balls into batter shaking off excess. Deep fry a few at a time in hot oil until golden brown, for about 3-4 minutes. Drain for a bit on paper towels and serve hot.

Rockfish Soufflé

It's a rarity to come across a French soufflé on today's contemporary menus, but interest in French cooking soared in the '70s with the help of Julia Child's cooking shows and books. This soufflé combines traditional French methods for making soufflés with rockfish, Maryland's official state fish. I love the magical presentation of a soufflé, and this savory version from Thompson's is easy to whip up in your own kitchen. Serve with a tossed salad and call it dinner. Who knows, maybe the soufflé is poised for a comeback.

Serves 6 (about ¾ cup each)

+ **1 ½ cups** milk
+ **2 cups** rockfish (striped bass), cooked, cooled, and flaked
+ **1 cup** dry breadcrumbs from day old bread
+ **1 teaspoon** butter
+ **4** egg yolks
+ **¼ teaspoon** seafood seasoning
+ **1/8 teaspoon** paprika
+ **4 drops** hot pepper sauce
+ **½ teaspoon** salt
+ **4** egg whites

Preheat oven to 350°F. In a heavy bottomed saucepan scald milk over low heat. Stir in the rockfish, breadcrumbs and butter. In a large bowl beat the egg yolks until thick. Stirring constantly, add the fish mixture into the egg yolks, a little at a time. Mix in seafood seasoning, paprika, and hot pepper sauce. In a small bowl, add salt to egg whites; beat to form softly rounded peaks (like shaving cream consistency). Fold egg whites into fish mixture.

Prepare a deep 6-to-8 inch baking dish with non-stick cooking spray and pour in the mixture. Set the baking dish in a pan containing hot water to cover 2/3 of baking dish. Bake for about one hour, until knife inserted in the center comes out clean. Serve immediately.

Oysters Florentine

Brunch anyone? Or maybe the holiday buffet table. This perfect little casserole served with glasses of champagne might just become a part of your holiday tradition. At smaller gatherings, place it on the coffee table with small bread-and-butter plates and cocktail forks.

Serves 4 to 6

+ **Two 10-ounce packages** frozen spinach
+ **1 pint** shucked Maryland select oysters, well drained
+ **¼ cup (½ stick)** butter or margarine
+ **¼ cup** flour
+ **1 ½ cups** milk

+ **½ cup** dry white wine
+ **½ cup** chopped scallions
+ Salt and pepper, to taste
+ Paprika
+ **1 cup** shredded Cheddar cheese

Preheat oven to 350°F. Thaw spinach and squeeze the moisture out. In a shallow 2-quart baking dish spread spinach and top with the oysters. Melt butter in a small saucepan. Stir in flour and cook for 30 seconds. Gradually, add milk, wine and scallions. Cook over low heat while stirring constantly until sauce reaches a boil and thickens. Add salt and pepper and enough paprika to create a rosy hue. Bake until hot and bubbly, about 30 minutes. Serve hot.

Thompson's Shrimp Scampi

Thompson's style scampi was presented with the tails still on and served with green beans and either rice pilaf or pasta.

Serves 4 as a main dish or 8 as an appetizer

+ **1 ½ pounds** jumbo shrimp, peeled and deveined
+ **7 tablespoons** butter, divided
+ 3 cloves garlic, finely chopped
+ **3 to 4 tablespoons** dry white wine
+ **¼ cup** fresh lemon juice
+ **1 teaspoon** seafood seasoning
+ **2 tablespoons** heavy cream
+ Salt and pepper, to taste

Melt half the butter over medium heat in a skillet. Add shrimp and garlic and cook, stirring until fragrant, about 2 minutes. Add wine, lemon juice, seafood seasoning and cream. Continue to stir and simmer for 4 minutes. Remove shrimp and keep warm. Boil the remaining ingredients for 3 minutes. Add reserved butter and season with salt and pepper, to taste. Before serving, return shrimp to sauce.

Baltimore County and Beyond

Brentwood Inn

Neighborhood: Dundalk

6700 Brentwood Avenue

Open: 1945 - 1982

For more than 30 years the family-owned Brentwood Inn was the place to celebrate birthdays, anniversaries, first communions and high school prom nights. At this Dundalk institution general manager and International Wine Sommelier, Joe Czernikowski, would greet and entertain guests with his arsenal of antics. "Your Congenial Host" mixed mammoth-sized cocktails for dinner guests all dispensed from a cart called "Joe's Welcome Wagon," which he personally wheeled from table to table. While reciting jokes, this self-described "master mixologist" threw shakers in the air and juggled glasses, before catching a couple of olives or cherries simultaneously in different stemmed glasses. Then he would place the glass up to your lips while filling it with a thin stream from the shaker he held over the top of your head with his left hand. He never missed.

In 1945, John J. Czernikowski, Joe's father, bought the small neighborhood tavern located on the corner of 5th Avenue and Brentwood. It was a small restaurant that offered tavern fare and seated 25. Over the years it grew to include two floors accommodating 300. Joe's wife, Dolores explained to the *Baltimore Sun* in 2003, "That was when Fort Holabird was booming. And the tavern was so successful they had to add more rooms." Not only did the restaurant grow, but so did the menu's offerings. The 10-page menu featured continental cuisine, American favorites, over 50 seafood selections and Chesapeake treats, and a smorgasbord on Tuesdays. It also listed the "Famous Brentwood Creations," which included its Beef Bourguignon topped with crunchy French-fried onions and Baked Seafood Imperial.

The Brentwood Inn was enormous, but it managed to maintain its neighborhood restaurant appeal. With signature accents of iron grillwork throughout, the décor was nautically themed. The cozy and relaxing Starlite Room had carpeting printed with starfish and conch shells. There were two larger dining rooms and one featured a large, mesmerizing aquarium and a giant red plastic lobster mounted on the wall.

Their spectacular wine cellar was stocked with 62,000 bottles including seven bottles of 1794 Madeira, a favorite of George Washington. In 1972 Joe would sell you a bottle for $500. Guests were encouraged to visit the famous cellar and select their wines while their dinner was being prepared. It was not to be missed! Every inch of ceiling space and every nook-and-cranny were covered in business cards and for many years served as the background for ads placed in *Gourmet Magazine*.

Although Joe Czernikowski ran a tight ship, his cheerful staff were enthusiastic and found him easy to work for. Sadly, the restaurant fell on poor economic times and was sold at auction to pay off debt while the contents of its famous wine cellar were later auctioned off to the public.

Postcard view of the internationally famous wine cellar at the Brentwood Inn, c. 1960s. *Author's collection.*

Hot Buttered Rum

A comfort drink if ever there was one, from John M. Czernikowski, one of Joe's sons. This holiday drink, sometimes called a hot toddy, starts with a buttery batter of sweet spices; the result is sweet, rich and indulgent.

Makes at least 20 drinks

+ **1 pound** high quality unsalted butter, room temperature

+ **1 teaspoon** ground cloves

+ **1 teaspoon** ground cinnamon

+ **1 teaspoon** ground nutmeg

+ **½ teaspoon** vanilla extract

+ **1 pound** brown sugar

+ Spiced Rum

To make the batter, beat the first five ingredients until fluffy. Continue to beat while adding the brown sugar. Refrigerate until ready to use.

To make a hot buttered rum, place a heaping tablespoon of batter in a mug. Fill the mug one-quarter full of rum. Fill the rest with steaming hot water. Stir until batter is dissolved. Garnish with a small pat of butter.

Hersh's Orchard Inn

Neighborhood: Towson

1528 East Joppa Road

Open: 1947 - 1997

For the uninitiated, restaurant reviewers often dubbed the Orchard Inn as "the Danny's of Towson," "the Prime Rib North" and "the suburban cousin of the Chesapeake." The upscale restaurant, seen by many as a Saturday night kind of place, was situated on a busy stretch of Joppa Road, but the minute you entered the building it was easy to forget about its commercial surroundings. For decades, the Orchard Inn had been a favorite dining spot for a faithful, older clientele, my grandparents included. A farmhouse inn and restaurant, it first opened in 1947 on a property bordering an apple orchard. Set back from the main road, its owners would eventually build a new restaurant complete with a traditional inn-like exterior closer to Joppa Road just west of Loch Raven Boulevard. Over the years, ownership changed hands several times with each owner bowing to tradition by keeping the old name. In 1979, Hersh Pachino, former manager of the Pimlico Hotel, bought the venerable restaurant and lounge and designated it Hersh's Orchard Inn.

That is how I remember it. My grandmother often took us there for dinner and I can recall that my family enjoyed at least one Christmas Eve dinner at the Orchard. It was a large restaurant seating about 250 in three dining rooms (Candlelight, Nautical and Coach), two banquet rooms, and an extremely popular piano lounge. Following a complete renovation, it took on a more sophisticated art deco-vibe.

I remember it as quite glamorous. My grandmother usually reserved a table in the Candlelight Room, the most formal of the three dining rooms. It was decorated in earth tones with lots of mirrors. The tables were surrounded by plush grey banquettes that you could comfortably sink into. It was the place for people watching because you just never knew who you might see. Almost like a throwback, I envisioned that old Hollywood-style practice of the maître d' delivering a telephone to the table of some bigwig awaiting that ever-important phone call. Dimly lit rooms had strategically placed vases of white gladiolas throughout. Live music filtered in from the lounge adding to the overall elegance. Early on, Pachino hired one of Baltimore's best pianists, Lawson Vessels. Patrons gathered around the grand piano as he entertained them with standards in the old style. After his death, changing times ushered in a new, younger clientele, and his spot at the keyboards was taken over by pianist, Ron DeFilippo, who played more contemporary pop tunes.

The lengthy menu offered mostly American dishes with an emphasis on seafood and, especially classic Maryland fare. On Thursday nights, diners could indulge in Maine lobster at reduced prices. Even costly stone crab claws were available during season, a rarity in these parts. It could be rather expensive, but it did not have to be because of the variety of daily specials that were printed inside the menu.

The walls of the small foyer were lined with framed photographs of visiting celebrities and sports stars who had dined there. It was fun to view the gallery of familiar show biz images while you were waiting to be taken to your table. Mr. Pachino kept a camera handy to photograph famous diners such as Joe DiMaggio, Sammy Davis Jr., Henny Youngman, Tom Selleck, Chris Evert, Martina Navratilova, Billy Dee Williams and many former Orioles players, including his good friend, Jim Palmer. It did not matter if you were a celebrity or the average Joe; Hersh Pachino was going to take good care of you. Palmer once said, "The restaurant was successful because of the guy who owned it. He understood people and the restaurant business." That he surely did. Pachino was named Restaurateur of the Year (in 1985) by the Restaurant Association of Maryland. Service and a competent kitchen were always the hallmark of the Orchard Inn and its success may have been its ability to keep on evolving, never staying stuck in the past.

Me, my father Tom Howell, and his wife Aliceann, visit the lounge at Hersh's Orchard Inn before our dinner reservation, c. 1987.

Gazpacho Soup

This chilled raw tomato-vegetable soup classic originated in southern Spain. Today there are many variations of the dish, and it is often seen on menus, particularly in hot summer months. At the Orchard Inn it was served in a cocktail glass and garnished with a large wedge of crisp cucumber.

Serves 6

+ 1 clove chopped garlic
+ 1 peeled cucumber, seeded and diced
+ 1 green pepper, seeded and diced
+ 2 hard cooked eggs, diced
+ 2 medium onions, finely diced
+ 2 ripe tomatoes, peeled and diced
+ **Two 10-ounce cans** condensed tomato soup
+ **2 soup cans** water
+ **¼ cup** fresh lemon juice
+ **1 teaspoon** salt
+ dash Tabasco sauce
+ **2 tablespoons** olive oil
+ **½ cup** buttered croutons

Rub soup tureen with chopped garlic and discard garlic. Place cucumber, green pepper, tomatoes, onions, and eggs in tureen. Mix tomato soup with water and add to tureen with the remaining ingredients, mixing well. Chill until icy cold. To serve, place an ice cube in individual bowls before adding soup and topping with croutons.

As a variation, mix all liquid ingredients and seasonings together and chill. Place the diced vegetables, chopped eggs and croutons in small bowls and allow each person to garnish his own soup.

Crab Fritters

These addictive appetizers are perfect for serving with cocktails at an informal get-together, or even as the centerpiece of a holiday buffet table. Be sure not to crowd the fryer; only cook about five fritters at a time. Slide them gently into the hot oil taking care not to drop them from a height that could make the oil splash.

Makes 24 fritters

Fritters:

+ 1 ¾ **cups** all-purpose flour
+ 1 ½ **cups** warm water
+ 2 **tablespoons** vegetable oil
+ 2 **teaspoons** baking powder
+ 1/8 **teaspoon** salt
+ 1 **pound** crabmeat
+ ¾ **cup** fresh white breadcrumbs
+ 4 large egg whites, divided
+ 3 **tablespoons** chopped fresh parsley
+ All-purpose flour for dredging
+ Vegetable oil, for deep frying
+ Curry Sauce, recipe follows

In a medium bowl, mix first five ingredients to blend. Allow the batter to sit for one hour at room temperature. In a large bowl, mix crabmeat, breadcrumbs, two egg whites and parsley. Season with salt and pepper. Divide the mixture into 24 mounds. Shape each mound firmly into a ball. Roll crabmeat ball in flour, shaking off the excess. Immediately before frying, in a small bowl beat remaining two egg whites to stiff peaks. Fold egg whites into batter.

Heat oil in deep fryer or heavy large saucepan to 360°F. Dip crab balls into batter one at a time, coating completely. Carefully lower into oil. Repeat with remaining crab balls, cooking until golden brown, turning frequently, for about five minutes. Using a slotted spoon, transfer fritters to paper towels and drain. Serve immediately with sauce.

Curry Sauce:

+ 1 ½ **tablespoons** olive oil
+ 1 small garlic clove, minced
+ 1 **teaspoon** curry powder
+ ½ **cup** mayonnaise
+ ½ **cup** sour cream
+ 2 **tablespoons** orange juice
+ 1 **tablespoon** sugar
+ 1 **tablespoon** fresh lemon juice
+ 1 **tablespoon** chutney

Heat oil in heavy small skillet over medium heat. Add garlic and sauté one minute. Add curry powder and stir for one minute. Transfer to a blender and add all remaining ingredients. Blend until smooth. Pour into a serving bowl.

Hersh's Orchard Inn Orange Creamsicle

Remember the flavor of Creamsicles when you were growing up? This summertime Orange Creamsicle cocktail is for the grown-up who misses that classic taste - enjoy!

Serves 1 (prepared in a 10-ounce glass)

+ **1 scoop** of orange sherbet
+ **1 ounce** white cocoa liqueur
+ **1 ounce** Licor 43

Blend with ice. Top with whipped cream. Indulge.

Dici Naz Velleggia

Neighborhood: Towson

204 East Joppa Road

Open: 1971 - 1993

The time was ripe for Nazzareno "Naz" Velleggia when he opened this offshoot of Little Italy's famous Velleggia's, the downtown restaurant his parents established in 1937. Popular with the over-30 crowd, Dici Naz Velleggia's was like a modern, upscale, neighborhood supper club that sophisticated suburbanites flocked to. People often asked (myself included), what "Dici Naz" meant. Velleggia told the *Baltimore Sun* it is Italian for, "say Naz." He added: "It's sort of like, 'say hey.' Dici Naz."

Like a party, it was packed nightly. Velleggia and his general manager, Johnny Dee (later owner of The Lounge in Parkville), made you feel special from the moment you walked in the door, according to my friend and longtime Dici Naz Velleggia's regular, Pat Thomas. She remembers many great times there and still misses it. "The atmosphere felt very New Yorkish to me...well-appointed with low lights and a great bar. Also, a dance floor that was well used with great talent playing a keyboard. It seemed that everyone there knew everyone else there, and Johnny Dee and Naz knew all of them and what they liked to eat and drink." Velleggia's had a cool, contemporary look and decidedly dressy tone, thanks to a dress code posted on the front door that required men to wear jackets after 5 p.m.

Located inside the Hampton House apartment building on the main floor facing Joppa Road; there was a stark contrast between the narrow hall leading to the restaurant and the attractive Mediterranean-like décor that unfolded inside. Large framed French antique posters, perhaps original lithographs, hung on the walls of the lobby and the lounge. Picture windows lined three sides of the large dining room that had been partitioned off into smaller, more intimate areas. Subtle lighting from a drop ceiling provided just the right ambiance, and views of a lit-up Towson were especially pretty after nightfall. Dark banquettes, plush carpeting, and well-spaced tables adorned with fresh carnations and tall candles set the mood, creating a comfortable dining experience.

The menu was classic Italian and similar to the original family restaurant, but it offered more continental style selections along with higher prices. In addition to homemade pastas and sauces, there were selections of steak, seafood and chicken, with an emphasis on veal. Dishes on the menu were named for staff and favorite customers. Semi-formally attired waitstaff were friendly, efficient and knowledgeable about the chef's daily specials.

There were not many places where you could have a nice dinner, and live background music, along with dancing afterward. With a dining area that spilled right onto the dance floor, there was always a crowd in the lounge because after-dinner diners would frequently gravitate to the bar for a nightcap or two. Yes indeed, Dici Naz Velleggia's was a playground for the local movers and shakers who came often and stayed late.

Jean Thomas and Pat Thomas (no relation) enjoy a "girls" night out at Dici Naz Velleggia's, c. 1984. Pat shared, "I never felt uncomfortable there since Johnny and Naz watched out for the ladies who were single."

Antipasto Caldo alla Velleggia

Hot Antipasto

This sampler of various hot hors d'oeuvres was a signature dish of the Velleggia family. Arranging a huge platter of antipasto is a little like creating your own masterpiece. Just begin with a large lettuce-lined platter and you have it made!

Serves 6 to 8

Italian Sausages

+ 5 Italian link sausages, pierced with a fork
+ 20 small mushroom caps, sautéed in butter
+ 20 small Italian pepperoncini (pickled green peppers)

Cut each sausage link into 4 pieces. Broil about 6 to 8 inches from the heat for about 20 minutes or until done. On a toothpick, place a piece of sausage followed by a sautéed mushroom cap and a pepperoncini. Continue in this manner until all the sausages, mushrooms and pepperoncini have been used. Before serving, place the toothpicks on a baking sheet and warm in a moderate oven.

Green Pepper

+ 1 medium green pepper
+ Anchovy filets
+ Finger lengths of Provolone cheese, cut ¼" thick.

Cut the green pepper into long strips, about ½-inch wide. Blanche in boiling water for 2 minutes. Drain in a colander and run cold water on top of the green pepper strips to stop their cooking and retain their color. Top each green pepper with an anchovy filet. Place a length of cheese on the anchovy filet. When ready to serve, place the peppers on a baking sheet and broil until the cheese has melted.

Clams Franco
A specialty of the house.

+ 12 cherrystone clams, cleaned and opened
+ Dash of olive oil
+ 2 jumbo shrimp, steamed
+ ¼ **pound** crabmeat
+ 2 **tablespoons** Italian breadcrumbs
+ 2 **tablespoons** chopped parsley
+ Old Bay seasoning
+ Salt and pepper, to taste
+ 1 egg, beaten
+ Marinara sauce or chopped canned tomatoes

Place the cherrystone clams in their half shells and sprinkle with a little olive oil. Chop the shrimp finely. Combine with crabmeat, breadcrumbs, parsley, Old Bay seasoning, salt and pepper. Add only enough egg to lightly bind the mixture together.

Divide the mixture among the clams, spreading it over the top of each one. Spoon a little marinara or chopped tomatoes on top of each crab mixture. Broil until heated through.

Sautéed Shrimp

+ **12** jumbo shrimp
+ **¼ cup** olive oil
+ Juice of ½ a lemon
+ **2 tablespoons** chopped parsley or fresh chopped **basil**
+ Salt and pepper, to taste

Peel and devein shrimp. In a skillet, add the olive oil and lemon juice. Heat until hot but not smoking. Add shrimp and sauté until they have turned pink, about 3 to 4 minutes. Sprinkle with chopped parsley or basil and season with salt and pepper to taste.

Eggplant

+ **1** small eggplant, peeled and cut into finger lengths
+ Egg Batter, recipe follows

Dip each eggplant finger into the batter and deep-fry until golden brown. Drain on paper towels and serve.

Egg Batter:

+ **1** egg
+ **¾ cup** water
+ **1 cup** flour
+ Salt and pepper, to taste
+ **1 teaspoon** oregano

Blend or whisk together until smooth. Let sit for 1 hour before using.

Saltimbocca alla Gino Marchetti

Legendary Baltimore Colts defensive end, Gino Marchetti and Naz Velleggia, were longtime friends. This was Gino's all-time favorite Velleggia's dish. Translated it means, "jumps in the mouth."

Serves 6

+ **2 pounds** veal scaloppini, about 6 large slices
+ 12 thin slices prosciutto ham
+ 12 thin slices mozzarella cheese
+ **3 tablespoons** olive oil
+ **2 tablespoons** butter
+ Flour
+ **½ cup** very finely chopped onions
+ **¾ cup** dry Marsala wine
+ **½ cup** chicken stock
+ Salt and pepper, to taste

With a flat mallet, pound meat to make thin slices about 8x4-inches. If they are too small, pound 2 or 3 together to form the proper size. Place enough ham and cheese over scaloppini to almost cover each oblong. Enclose the scaloppini as if folding a 3-part letter: Bring the bottom up to the middle and the top down over. Pound the ends together. (This can be done a day ahead).

In a skillet, heat together the olive oil and butter. Dust each veal package in a little flour and quickly sauté. When they are golden brown on one side, turn them over. Add chopped onions to the skillet and stir. Toward the end of browning the second side, add the Marsala and stock to the pan.

When the scaloppini packages are golden brown and cooked through, transfer them to a warm serving platter. Reduce the sauce, if necessary, until it is the consistency of au jus. Season with salt and pepper. Pour over the veal and serve.

Green Bean Salad

I enjoy serving something green at dinnertime, and this marinated salad is one that you can prepare ahead. It keeps for a few days in the refrigerator and the flavor gets more delicious the longer it sits.

Serves 6

+ 1 ½ **pounds** green beans, trimmed
+ 1 small red onion, chopped
+ Salt and pepper
+ Olive oil
+ Red wine vinegar

Cook the beans in a pot of boiling, salted water until al dente, about 3 to 4 minutes. Drain in a colander and run cold water over them to stop the cooking and to maintain their green color. Toss the beans and red onion with salt and pepper to taste.

Prepare a dressing of 1 part vinegar to 2 parts oil. Toss with the desired amount of dressing to taste.

Country Fare Inn

Neighborhood: Reisterstown (1973 - 1977)
                Owings Mills (1977 - 1990)

100 Painters Mill Road

Open: 1973 - 1990

*J*ust outside of historic Reisterstown on Westminster Pike, an old white wooden house stands. It once served as a stagecoach stop, but in 1973, this rustic building with its knotty-pine interior became home to a charming new French restaurant, the Country Fare Inn. Previously, the Country Fare Inn had been a fried chicken and corn-on-the-cob type of establishment, and its new owners had agreed to retain the name. Richard Pirone had teamed up with his old friend, Stuart Teper, and they would go on to become hugely influential in developing the Baltimore restaurant scene. The Country Fare Inn was a pioneer of true French cuisine in Maryland. Together they formulated a novel business model that featured a three-way owner/management system - a host, a chef and a restaurant administrator. Building on the success of this model, Messrs. Pirone and Teper formed a consortium, the Country Fare Group, whose holdings included among others, the Brass Elephant, King's Contrivance, Fiori, and City Lights. Mr. Pirone enjoyed creating cozy little getaways where diners could relax and leave the outside world behind. Initially, Roland Jeannier, a talented and well-respected chef rounded out the establishment's team. Hailing from southern France, he had established himself in Baltimore, but it was while he ran the kitchen at the Country Fare that he would really make a name for himself.

About four years later an opportunity for expansion presented itself, and the restaurant was moved to a more elegant setting, the Samuel Owings house, known as Ulm, in Owings Mills. An architectural gem, the 18th century brick colonial house had been named for Owings' three mills, the upper, lower, and middle, using the first letter of each to form the acronym. Built around 1767 and beautifully restored in 1970, it retained wide-board floors, fireplaces with hand-carved mantles and even a stone wine cellar. Once inside the doors, it was easy to forget that you were situated within the confines of an industrial park.

With its sophisticated, yet old-fashioned surroundings (think Williamsburg) and discreet lighting, the venue was ideal for celebrating a special occasion or romantic evening. Many moons ago, I went on my first "formal" dinner date at the Country Fare Inn. I am not sure that I had even heard of it before, but he had invited me out, making all the arrangements for a memorable evening and I felt extremely flattered. I spent hours primping and preening before the mirror and changing numerous times on a quest to find that perfect outfit! That evening my date arrived with a bouquet of flowers and informed me that his mother had asked that we stop by so she could take a couple of snapshots! We were young and I imagine she was simply curious to meet the young woman who her son was going to such lengths for! I enjoyed meeting his mother that night; she was warm and made me feel welcome and at ease. I remember her enthusiasm as she snapped away with her camera, satisfied that she had been successful in capturing the moment. I am now kicking myself for not requesting a copy!

We pulled up to this charming 18th century house whose covered front porch had been dramatically illuminated with floodlights. I could not wait to see the inside. It was this perfectly unpretentious little French restaurant with a couple of intimate dining rooms appointed with attractive curtains and muted walls. Candlelit tables set with fresh flowers and soft background music lent a romantic informality to the gracious setting. The well thought out menu was printed on a striking calligraphy scroll with offerings of peppercorn duck and Cornish game hens. We dined at a leisurely pace, enjoying our dinner; Mr. Pirone allowed for a two hour duration, which meant less turnover, and more difficulty in securing a coveted Saturday night reservation.

The servers were generally young and adept, though not professional waiters in the true sense. You knew you could count on a relaxed and pleasant evening with good, imaginative food at a fair price. Downstairs was a grotto-like stone wine cellar. Aptly named the Wine Cellar, it was a more casual option that offered light fare and popular acoustic entertainment. My date and I spent the remainder our evening in the Wine Cellar where we enjoyed live entertainment and, of course, a little wine. It was a truly magical evening. Over the years we lost track of each other and now, looking back on the fond memories I hold of that night, I hope that I gave him an inkling of the great impression he made on me. After all, it was his gift of time and effort that made me feel so special. Bring back the art of the dinner date, please!

The Country Fare Inn closed in 1990 and Fiori, already a veteran of the Baltimore County dining scene, was reborn in the Samuel Owings location after many years of operation out on Westminster Pike. Ah yes, history often repeats itself.

Tomatoes Mentonnaise

Menton lies on the eastern French Riviera near the Italian border. Mentonnaise is the name for a variety of regional garnishes inspired by the Provençal style of cooking.

Serves 4

+ 4 medium ripe tomatoes
+ 4 hard-boiled eggs

+ 4 to 6 anchovies

Cut tomatoes in half crosswise. Gently squeeze to remove the seeds. Push the yolks and anchovies through a strainer so they become smooth and fill the tomatoes. To create the appearance of a daisy, julienne the egg whites and place the strips in the tomato halves to resemble the spokes of a wheel.

Phone (301) 833-2200

COUNTRY FARE INN

Continental Cuisine

808 Westminster Rd.
Route 140
Reisterstown, Maryland 21136

PLEASE CLOSE COVER—STRIKE ON BACK

Scallops Gauguin

Chef Jeannier considered this to be his specialty at the Country Fare Inn. On a trip to Tahiti he had been served marinated roe and came up with his own interpretation of the dish naming it for the famous painter who made French Polynesia his home in 1891.

Serves 4

+ **1 pound** sea scallops, sliced in halves or thirds, about the size of bay scallops
+ Juice of 1 lime
+ Milk of 1 coconut or ¼ cup canned coconut milk
+ 4 small young zucchini, sliced ¼" thick
+ **¼ pound** butter
+ **2 tablespoons** chopped parsley

Combine lime juice and coconut milk and marinate the scallops for 15 minutes. Sauté zucchini quickly in half the butter and season to taste with salt and pepper. Remove to a serving platter and keep warm. Heat a sauté pan over moderate heat and add the scallops and marinade. Cook quickly, just long enough to warm the scallops through. With a slotted spoon, arrange the scallops over the zucchini. Reduce the pan juices and emulsify with the remaining butter, adding it off heat. Pour the sauce over the scallops and serve by sprinkling with chopped parsley on top.

Le Canard au Poivre Vert

Roast Duck in Green Sauce

Serves 4

+ **1 duck, 4 to 5 pounds**
+ **2 tablespoons** green peppercorns in brine, drained and rinsed
+ **2 tablespoons** butter
+ **¼ cup** brandy
+ **1 tablespoon** flour
+ **1/3 cup** beef stock
+ **1 tablespoon** dry vermouth
+ **1/3 cup** chicken stock
+ **1 cup** heavy cream
+ **4 cups** cooked wild rice

Preheat oven to 475°F. Roast duck for one hour, basting with drippings occasionally. Remove from oven and cool. Cut the duck in half and remove breast bones, rib bones and leg bones. Finish cooking the duck halves at 325°F for 20 minutes in a roasting pan filled with enough water in the bottom to prevent sticking. Do not overcook.

For the sauce, melt butter in a skillet and sauté peppercorns for one minute. Add the brandy and ignite. Shake the pan until the alcohol burns off and set aside.

In a separate skillet, combine flour and beef stock and stir over moderate heat until it becomes a paste. Add vermouth and chicken stock and let it come to a boil, stirring constantly. Reduce the mixture to half and stir this into the green peppercorns.

Add the heavy cream, salt and pepper to taste, and whisk to incorporate. Reduce slightly. Slice duck and serve over wild rice, with the sauce ladled over the top.

Cornish Game Hens with Chestnuts

Serves 4

+ **4** Cornish game hens
+ *Pork Farce*, recipe follows
+ **¼ pound** butter
+ **½ pound** whole chestnuts from Pork Farce

+ **1 cup** water or dry white wine
+ Bouquet of watercress
+ Steamed potatoes, optional

Preheat oven to 350°F. Clean the hens and prepare for stuffing. Prepare the *Pork Farce* for stuffing the hens.

Place the hens in a roasting pan and dot with butter. Arrange the chestnuts around the hens along with any leftover stuffing. Roast in oven for 20 minutes. Raise the oven temperature from 425°F to 450°F so the hens brown. Continue to roast for another 10 minutes or until stuffing is done. (Insert a fork - the juices should run clear, not red.)

Arrange on a platter and surround with steamed potatoes, if desired. Deglaze the pan and place over moderate heat. Add water or wine and bring to a boil, scraping the bits off the bottom of the pan. The sauce can be reduced at this point, if desired. Pour over hens and garnish with watercress.

Pork Farce:

+ **1 pound** fresh chestnuts
+ **1 pound** mild, ground sausage meat

+ Pinch of thyme

Preheat oven to 450°F. Make an x-shaped incision on the round side of each of the chestnuts. (This will prevent them from bursting in the oven.) Roast in a hot oven for 10 to 15 minutes or until the shells break apart when squeezed. The chestnuts should be soft to the touch. Peel all chestnuts and crumble half of them into chunks. (Reserve the remaining chestnuts for the game hens.) Mix crumbled chestnuts with sausage, thyme, salt and pepper to taste.

Fiori

Neighborhood: Reisterstown (1977 - 1990)
Owings Mills (1990 - 1995)

100 Painters Mill Road

Open: 1977 - 1995

There was a time when most Baltimoreans only associated Italian restaurants with Little Italy. That perception changed when the Country Fare Group consortium opened Fiori restaurant, first in the one-time Reisterstown stagecoach stop out on Westminster Pike that dated back to 1722 and had previously been occupied by the Country Fare Inn. Word caught on and folks were willing to make the 40-minute drive from Baltimore because there was unprecedented and growing interest in authentic, regional Italian cooking across America.

According to the menu, the concept behind Fiori read: "Italy's history had been one of independent tribes, cities and kingdoms until the country was invited in 1870 into one nation. Despite the unification, an intense local patriotism became part of the Italian character. This regional feeling produced an independent people and an infinite variety of foods. Here is the inspiration for the Fiori regional concept of Italian cooking." From the red marinara sauces of the south to the cream sauces of the north; there was something for every appetite at Fiori.

Fast forward to 1990 and the closure of the Country Fare Inn. That's when Fiori reopened in its new home in the Georgian two-story brick Samuel Owings house perched on a bluff overlooking the intersection of Painter's Mill and Dolfield Roads in Owings Mills. Some found the colonial Williamsburg style décor wasn't the right fit for Italian cuisine, but many simply enjoyed knowing they were in for delicious fare and polished service in the pleasing surroundings of a beautiful and historic old home.

As you entered the foyer, you were greeted with an impressive dessert cart filled with a selection of hard to resist homemade desserts. This left patrons with an immediate desire to save room for later. Fiori's top-rate menu was intriguing and mouthwatering: how was one to choose from mussels a la marinara, pork chops and peppers, a variety of homemade pastas, seafood, and veal specialties? Salads were always fresh with hand-sliced romaine leaves topped with either the delicious Fiori house dressing or the Roquefort dressing for which the restaurant had become known. And, thankfully for us, through the years the management team was most generous in their attitude of sharing house recipes so that we could try to duplicate the dishes in our own kitchens and share them with our loved ones. Sadly, it would seem the historic 18th century Samuel Owings house no longer fit the setting of the surrounding Painters Mill Executive Park and in 1996 it was razed to make way for a $20 million office tower and parking garage.

Fiori's Rice Croquettes

Arancini aka Rice Balls

Makes 4 to 6 servings (12-16 croquettes)

+ **1 cup** white rice**
+ **2 cups** water
+ **¾ to 1 cup** bechamel (white) sauce, using packaged mix
+ **2 eggs**
+ Salt and white pepper
+ **¼ cup** Parmesan cheese, or to taste
+ Flour, eggs, and breadcrumbs for breading
+ Vegetable oil, for frying

Prepare rice so that it's sticky. Follow directions on the bechamel packaging and cook the sauce until thick, like wallpaper paste. Put rice in a bowl and strain the bechamel gradually into the rice so that it is not soupy. It should resemble rice pudding.

Coddle the eggs by boiling enough water to cover the eggs, slipping them into the water, removing the pan from heat and standing for 6 minutes. The shells and white will peel away, leaving the yolk intact and still soft.

Add the yolks, salt, white pepper and Parmesan cheese to the rice-bechamel mixture. Place in the refrigerator and allow to cool for 15 minutes. Shape the mixture by hand into medium-size balls. Coat balls in flour, beaten egg yolk, and then coat in breadcrumbs. Refrigerate again for 15-20 minutes. Deep fry until crisp and brown draining on paper towels. Serve in a pool of marinara sauce or on the side.

**Note: For best results cook rice the day before and refrigerate.

Fiori's Marinara Sauce

This is a staple sauce that freezes very well. It can be used with pasta, chicken, scallops and mussels.

Makes 4 quarts

+ **½ cup** olive oil
+ ½ medium yellow onion, chopped
+ **8** cloves garlic, peeled and cracked
+ **Four 28-ounce cans** Italian plum tomatoes (not in puree), preferably San Marzano
+ **½ cup** to **¾ cup** Chablis
+ Salt and pepper, to taste
+ **½ tablespoon** oregano
+ **½ tablespoon** basil
+ **½ teaspoon** marjoram
+ **¼ teaspoon** rosemary
+ Hot pepper flakes, to taste

Heat the olive oil in a heavy Dutch oven. Sauté onion until golden brown and slightly caramelized. Remove the onions and set aside. Cut the ends off the garlic cloves and sauté until golden brown. Add tomatoes that have been crushed by hand, and the onions. Bring to a boil and skim off any foam that comes to the top. Add wine. Bring back to a boil and skim again, if necessary.

Season with salt, pepper, oregano, basil, marjoram, rosemary and hot pepper flakes. Bring to a boil again and reduce to a simmer. Cook for about 20 minutes until slightly reduced and thickened.

Fiori's House Salad

Serves 4

+ ¼ head romaine, torn into bite-size pieces
+ ¼ head red-leaf lettuce, torn into bite-size pieces
+ ¼ **head** iceberg lettuce, torn into bite-size pieces
+ ¼ head escarole, torn into bite-size pieces
+ Small handful of black and green olives
+ 3 medium tomatoes, quartered
+ 1 small cucumber, sliced
+ 1 small red onion, sliced
+ **1 cup** Fiori Dressing (see next page)

Place lettuces in a salad bowl and garnish with olives, tomatoes, cucumber and onion. Toss with the dressing.

Fiori's Dressing

I was a teenager when Cuisinart introduced its first food processor. It was not too long before my mother unboxed one of her own, and enthusiastically demonstrated for me just how versatile this powerhouse device really was. I happened to enter the kitchen one afternoon when she was experimenting with making some homemade mayonnaise. It was like a science project. I was amazed that she could take such everyday kitchen staples as oil, egg yolks and some lemon juice, whiz them around and come up with mayonnaise! Who knew? This recipe is called a dressing, but it doubles as a homemade mayonnaise. Use any neutral oil, just make sure that the eggs are at room temperature so that they will emulsify nicely.

Makes 4 cups

+ 2 anchovies
+ 2 cloves garlic, peeled
+ 2 eggs, room temperature
+ **2 cups** salad oil
+ **1 cup** olive oil
+ **½ teaspoon** lemon juice

+ **6 tablespoons** red wine vinegar
+ Worcestershire sauce, to taste
+ Paprika, to taste
+ Salt and pepper, to taste

Mash the anchovies and garlic in a food processor. Add the eggs and beat for 1 to 2 minutes until creamy. Gradually, add the oils through the feeding tube, blending until it forms an emulsion. Beat in lemon juice, red wine vinegar and seasonings. Store in an air-tight container and refrigerate until ready for use.

My mother, Ann Howell, c. 1974.

Fiori's Roquefort Dressing

Makes 1 cup

+ **1 cup** sour cream
+ **1 to 2 tablespoons** mayonnaise
+ **1 ounce** half-and-half
+ **½ teaspoon** garlic, crushed
+ **¼ teaspoon** salt
+ Pinch of cayenne pepper
+ White pepper, to taste
+ **4 ounces** Roquefort cheese

With a hand mixer, combine sour cream and mayonnaise. Slowly add in half-and-half until well mixed. Add garlic, salt, cayenne pepper and white pepper, mixing until all ingredients are fully incorporated. Stir in the cheese; cover and refrigerate until ready to serve.

Linguini with White Clam Sauce

Serves 4

+ **2 dozen** cherrystone clams, cleaned
+ **¾ pound** imported thin linguini
+ **4 to 5** cloves garlic, peeled and smashed
+ **½ cup** extra virgin olive oil
+ **¼ cup** dry white wine
+ Salt and pepper, to taste
+ **½ teaspoon** dried basil
+ **¼ teaspoon** dried oregano
+ Large pinch of red pepper flakes
+ **3 tablespoons** chopped parsley
+ **4 tablespoons** butter (optional)

Over a bowl, shuck the clams, reserving the juice, then chop clams coarsely and set aside. Cook pasta al dente, according to packaging. Drain. Brown the garlic in olive oil. Add reserved clam juice and bring to a boil, skimming off any foam that rises to the top. Add remaining ingredients except butter. Add clams to sauce and heat clams through. Off heat, whisk in butter, if desired. Place pasta in a serving dish and mix some of the sauce in and pour remaining sauce over top.

Pork Chops with Vinegar Peppers

I love making my own fresh and colorful brined peppers, but if time does not permit you can find jarred red peppers in brine at the grocery store. This quick and tasty meal is sure to become a weeknight favorite when pork chops are calling your name.

Serves 4

+ Peppers in vinegar brine, recipe follows
+ **2 to 3 tablespoons** olive oil
+ **Eight 1" thick** pork loin chops, trimmed
+ **1 tablespoon** butter
+ **2 large shallots,** chopped
+ **6 peppercorns,** freshly cracked
+ **¼ cup** white wine

Pour off ½ cup of vinegar brine and set aside. Coat the bottom of an ovenproof skillet with olive oil and brown the chops very quickly. Drain and set aside. Add butter to skillet and sauté shallots and peppercorns for 1 minute. Deglaze pan with reserved vinegar brine and white wine. Return chops to the pan. Remove the equivalent of 2 julienned red peppers from the vinegar brine and add to the chops. Bring contents of the skillet to a simmer and place skillet in a 350°F oven for 15 minutes and serve.

Peppers in vinegar brine:

+ **4 or more** green peppers
+ **4 or more** red peppers
+ **2 teaspoons** salt
+ White distilled vinegar
+ Dry white wine and water to equal half the vinegar

Cut peppers into julienne pieces, removing all seeds and white membrane. Place in salted, distilled vinegar to cover. Add wine and water. Bring to a fast boil and let simmer for 3 to 5 minutes. Remove from heat and pack into sterilized Mason jars. Under refrigeration, they will keep several weeks.

Green Beans Margherita

Serves 4

+ **1 ½ pounds** green beans
+ **1** small onion, finely chopped
+ **3 tablespoons** butter
+ Salt and pepper, to taste
+ **½ cup** chicken broth
+ **2 ounces** chopped prosciutto ham

Blanch the beans in boiling salted water until al dente, about 2 minutes. Drain in a colander and run cold water over them to stop their cooking and retain their bright green color. This can be done ahead of time and beans placed in refrigerator.

Sauté the onions in butter until translucent. When ready to serve, return beans to pan and season with salt and pepper. Add broth and prosciutto. Sauté in the pan until the broth and butter evaporate and glaze the beans.

Fiori's Chocolate Sabayon

Sabayon is a classic Italian dessert. This incredibly creamy custard is made even more decadent with the addition of chocolate, raspberry and Cointreau - need I say more?

Serves 6

+ **1 cup** heavy whipping cream
+ **3** egg yolks
+ **2 ounces** sugar
+ **3 tablespoons** Cointreau
+ **1 teaspoon** plain gelatin

+ **¼ cup** hot water
+ **2 ounces** semi-sweet chocolate, melted
+ **6 teaspoons** raspberry preserves

Whip cream to soft peaks and set aside in refrigerator. In a separate mixing bowl, whisk together egg yolks, sugar, and Cointreau. Place in a double boiler over hot - not boiling - water and whisk, turning pan continually until candy thermometer reaches 110 degrees. Remove from heat immediately and continue whipping until mixture reaches room temperature.

Combine gelatin and hot water and stir until completely dissolved. Whisk gelatin mixture into egg mixture and stir until well mixed. Add chocolate, whisking until combined. Carefully fold in whipped cream, being careful not to break down the cream. Line six 6-ounce dessert glasses with raspberry preserves and fill glasses equally with chocolate mixture. Refrigerate.

Italian Cheesecake

Serves 6 to 8

+ **4** eggs
+ **¾ cup** sugar
+ **2 teaspoons** vanilla extract

+ **2 tablespoons** Anisette liqueur
+ **2 pounds** ricotta cheese, well drained

Preheat oven to 325°F. Butter well and flour a 9-inch springform pan. Beat together eggs, sugar and vanilla until light in color and doubled in bulk. Beat in Anisette. Break up ricotta cheese and add to egg mixture (do not worry if ricotta appears lumpy). Pour batter into prepared pan and bake for 1 to 1 ¼ hours or until brown on top. Allow to cool completely, then release springform. Cake will keep fresh for about 3 days under refrigeration, although it is best on the day prepared. Serve with espresso coffee.

Milton Inn

Neighborhood: Sparks

14833 York Road

Open: 1 9 4 7 - 2 0 2 0

*I*t is incredibly difficult to write about the Milton Inn in the past tense; the wound is still fresh. My heart broke upon learning that it had been permanently closed. This beloved place that had always been a part of my life, suddenly no longer existed. On June 12, 2020, chef/proprietor Brian Boston announced the closure in a letter he posted to the restaurant's website. It was a casualty of the Covid-19 pandemic. Not surprisingly, messages full of memories and regrets poured in on social media feeds. This historic treasure in northern Baltimore County—one of the region's most iconic restaurants— had entered 2020 celebrating its 73rd year.

A genteel, country, fine-dining destination three miles north of Shawan Road, the Milton Inn was housed in a fieldstone residence built around 1740. Rich in history, the Inn was originally a stagecoach stop for Quakers who traveled to monthly religious services down the road at the New Gunpowder Meeting House. In the 19th century it became home to the Milton Academy, a posh boy's school once attended by presidential assassin John Wilkes Booth. The Academy was named for John Milton, the English poet and author of *Paradise Lost*. It served as a school for many years, later housing several businesses until it became a restaurant in 1947. The Milton Inn had several owners, including Attilio and Eleanora Allori, who bought the place in 1959. The Alloris first met in Little Italy at Maria's "300" restaurant, where Attilio had been in partnership with his cousin's wife, Maria. Eleanora had a job there as a hat check girl. As operators of the Inn for a quarter century, Mr. Allori prepared meals in the kitchen while Mrs. Allori worked the front of the house, greeting guests. They made you feel at home. Customers delighted in architectural charm while enjoying a wide range of elegant Italian, French and American classics that everyone in the '60s considered *de rigueur*: escargot, oysters Rockefeller, Tournedos Rossini, Chateaubriand, Steak Diane, Lobster Newburg, red snapper Livornese and Duck a l'Orange. Service was well-paced, never hurried and diners could enjoy their meals in a relaxed, yet formal setting. After her husband's death in 1979, Mrs. Allori continued operating the restaurant until her retirement in 1987. She sold the business to local commercial real estate developer, Clarke F. Mackenzie, and several associates.

A succession of fine chefs earned the Milton Inn a national reputation for elegant, continental dining. These included noted Maryland chef, Mark Henry, who had done his turn as a sous chef at the glamorous Rainbow

Room on the 65th floor of Rockefeller Plaza in New York City. In 1977 my parents took my sisters and me there for dinner and dancing (complete with a big band orchestra). The experience was magical, one that I will *never* forget. What an extraordinary place to hone one's culinary skills! During Henry's 6 ½ years at the Milton Inn, he brought the place national recognition. *Esquire* magazine named him one of America's best young chefs, and *Conde Nast Traveler* listed the Inn among the top 50 restaurants in the United States. Known for his sauces and culinary surprises, Henry overhauled the menu to include interesting and imaginative dishes.

Henry left when he had the opportunity to open his own restaurant on the Eastern Shore, and in 1997 Baltimore County native, Brian Boston, took the reins as executive chef and operating partner. This talented Culinary Institute of America graduate was classically trained in French cuisine. Boston had begun as a line cook at Peerce's Plantation then later worked as a sous chef at the Brass Elephant. At the Milton Inn he carried on the tradition of excellence, helping the restaurant earn the prestigious DiRoNA (Distinguished Restaurant of North America) award for exemplifying the highest quality in dining and hospitality based on cuisine, service and atmosphere. It was the only Baltimore County restaurant to receive it. The Inn also got the 5-Star Diamond award from the American Academy of Hospitality Services.

The Inn was surrounded by trees and well-tended gardens. Walking through the doors of the charming country house transported visitors to a colonial atmosphere. Here they found six elegantly appointed dining rooms decorated with period furnishings, equestrian décor and five fireplaces. Most popular among returning customers were the Main Dining Room just to the right inside the entrance, and the Hearth Room.

Over the years I probably dined in every one of the dining rooms at least once. My dad and stepmom liked entertaining family and friends at the Inn, and over the years we celebrated many birthdays and anniversaries there, sometimes upstairs in the private dining room. My father celebrated what turned out to be his final birthday at the Milton Inn in 2014, by throwing a private gathering. While fondly reminiscing the other day with my Aunt Diane, we enjoyed a chuckle about the time her high heel shoe went right through a crack in the original wide-board flooring!

The Hearth Room situated in the rear was originally the house's kitchen. It was highlighted by a huge wood-burning stone fireplace that they lit when the outside temperature dropped below 30 degrees. The Inn's tables were always beautifully set with fresh flowers and sparkling stemware reflecting candlelight from illuminated hurricane lanterns. In my experience the service was always impeccable. They built their contemporary American menu around locally sourced produce according to the season. The kitchen staff did their own butchering, and the most popular item on the menu was The Filet of Chesapeake: filet mignon, crab cake with béarnaise sauce, Jack Tarr potatoes and seasonal vegetables—simple but executed with perfection. The wine cellar featured 200 handpicked selections, and the dessert pastries were all made in-house.

The Milton Inn was always a popular destination for special occasions and celebrations; a romantic place for that special dinner-for-two, or a place to woo clients on an expense account. Countless couples who got engaged there came back year after year to celebrate anniversaries and other milestones. But as the public has become more casual, fine dining restaurants have had to evolve.

Boston set out to change the expensive, special-occasion mindset the Inn inspired. He wanted it to also be a friendly neighborhood restaurant, so he expanded the lounge to include the formerly separate Fox and Hearth Rooms. This new room was named: the 1740 Lounge. In addition to burgers, sandwiches and salads, Boston introduced a moderately priced 26-item small-plates menu.

The world is changing very quickly. As of summer, 2020, the long term effects of the coronavirus remain to be seen. Fine dining is ultimately built around an intimate, in-person dining experience, and let's face it, take-out and delivery isn't the same. I am, by nature, an optimistic person and I would like to think that there is a silver lining, but the question remains: how will fine dining be re-imagined? What will the new culinary world look like?

Milton Inn "Paradise Lost" Oysters

The National Oyster Cook-off is held each year during the St. Mary's County Oyster Festival in Leonardtown, Maryland. At the 26th annual cook-off in 2006, chef Boston won first place in the Hors d'oeuvres division for this incredible dish. Although the name, Paradise Lost, is a reference to Milton's poem, it now seems strangely fitting.

Serves 4 to 6

+ **12** Maryland oysters on the half shell
+ **1 tablespoon** butter
+ **1** ear fresh corn, smoked and cut off the cob
+ **¼ cup** sliced shitake mushrooms
+ **½** tomato, skinned and seeded, cut into small dice
+ **2 tablespoons** cooked and diced applewood smoked bacon
+ **½ cup** beurre blanc (recipe follows)
+ Fresh chopped parsley
+ Seaweed

Preheat oven to 400°F. Bake oysters until they pop open, about 4-6 minutes. Shuck and discard the top shell. In a small skillet, sauté the corn and mushrooms in butter. Add tomato, bacon and parsley. Stir to heat through. Top oysters with the corn mixture. Then top with smoked tomato beurre blanc. Serve over seaweed.

Beurre Blanc

+ **1 cup** white wine
+ **1 tablespoon** cracked peppercorns
+ **1** shallot, diced
+ **1** sprig fresh thyme
+ **¼ cup** heavy cream
+ **½ pound** butter
+ **¼ cup** smoked tomato puree
+ Fresh chopped parsley

Reduce together the first four ingredients. Add heavy cream and reduce until quite thick. Remove from heat, whip in butter and strain. Add smoked tomato puree and chopped parsley to taste.

Tom Voss' Favorite Oyster Stew

This recipe was named for Tom Voss, a horse trainer who lived in Monkton and frequented the Milton Inn. Voss died in 2014.

Serves 4 to 6

+ 3 slices bacon
+ **4 tablespoons (½ stick)** unsalted butter
+ **½ cup** finely chopped onion
+ **½ cup** finely chopped celery
+ **1 ½ tablespoons** flour
+ **1 quart** half-and-half
+ **1 pint** shucked oysters with liquor (juice), preferably Blue Points
+ Salt and black pepper
+ **1 ½ tablespoons** Old Bay seasoning
+ Worcestershire sauce

In a heavy medium pot, cook bacon over medium-high heat until crisp. Remove bacon and drain on paper towels (leaving rendered fat in the pot). Crumble bacon and set aside.

Add butter to bacon fat and melt over medium-low heat. Add chopped onion and celery and cook until soft, 10 minutes.

Add flour, stirring 1 minute to make a roux. Pour in half-and-half and the oyster liquor (reserving oysters). Season with salt and pepper, Old Bay and a couple dashes of Worcestershire. Cook over medium heat 5 minutes. Do not allow it to boil. This base can be prepared up to 1 day in advance. Cover and chill until ready to serve.

To serve: Reheat base (again, do not boil). Add oysters, cook 30 to 60 seconds. Ladle into individual bowls and top with bacon.

Salade Eleanora

Mrs. Allori created this salad which remained a menu staple for years. It was served with hot, crusty French bread.

Serves 4

+ 1 bunch watercress
+ 2 stalks hearts of palm, sliced and drained
+ ½ head of Belgian endive, washed
+ 2 large mushrooms, sliced
+ ½ Granny Smith apple, sliced
+ House Vinaigrette (recipe follows)

Wash watercress and trim away all but the leaves; place in salad bowl. Add hearts of palm, endive, mushrooms and apple. Toss to combine. Add House Vinaigrette and toss again.

House Vinaigrette
Yields over 2 cups

+ 2 egg yolks
+ 2 **tablespoons** Dijon mustard
+ 1 clove garlic, chopped
+ 2 **tablespoons** Parmesan cheese, grated
+ 2 **cups** olive oil
+ 5 ½ **ounces** red wine vinegar
+ Salt and white pepper to taste

Place the first four ingredients in a blender or food processor and blend. Through the feed tube, slowly add the olive oil. As mixture thickens, add vinegar, salt and pepper.

Melini Veal Chop with White Bean Ragout

The kitchen prepared this dish using Melini red wine and served it with dried tomatoes and roasted baby squash, baby zucchini and baby beets.

Serves 4

+ **1 cup** dried pinto beans
+ **6 cups** chicken stock, divided
+ **½ cup** julienned bacon
+ **1** carrot, finely diced
+ **2** stalks celery, finely diced
+ **¼** red onion, finely diced
+ Salt and pepper, to taste
+ **4 10-ounce** veal chops

+ **1 tablespoon** oil
+ **1** shallot, diced
+ **1 cup** red wine
+ **1 tablespoon** fresh thyme
+ **2 cups** veal stock
+ **1 tablespoon** fresh chives, chopped

Soak beans in 2 cups chicken stock overnight. Cook beans in remaining 4 cups stock until cooked through. In a large skillet, render bacon until it begins to brown. Add carrots, celery, red onions and cook for 2 minutes. Remove from heat. Strain beans and add to the vegetable mixture. Season with salt and pepper.

In the same pot cook shallots in oil. Deglaze with wine. When 90 percent of wine has evaporated, add thyme and veal stock. Reduce and add chives.

Preheat grill. Season veal chops with salt and pepper and grill to medium-rare. Spoon vegetable mixture onto plates, top with veal chops and drizzle with wine reduction.

Pan-Fried Rockfish with Crab Hash and Delmarva Salsa

Chef Henry suggested this colorful Chesapeake Bay dish for Marylanders who wanted to get creative with the state's bounty of fresh produce and local seafood.

Serves 12

+ **5 pounds** trimmed rockfish filet cut into 12 6-to-7 ounce portions
+ Peanut oil for pan frying
+ *Delmarva Salsa* (recipe follows)
+ *Crab Hash* (recipe follows)
+ **12 ounces** *Beurre Blanc* (recipe follows)
+ Lemon and fresh dill for garnish

Preheat skillet with 2 tablespoons oil. Brown fish filets on both sides until three-quarters done and remove from heat. Place the filets in oven pan. Heat salsa and crab hash. When both are hot, heat fish through under broiler being careful not to overcook. Place a thin bed of salsa on plate. Place crab hash on salsa, then place fish on crab hash. Top fish with beurre blanc, garnish and serve.

Delmarva Salsa

+ 1 medium Vidalia onion
+ 1 each yellow, green and red bell peppers (medium)
+ **2 tablespoons** peanut oil
+ 1 medium cucumber
+ 1 medium zucchini
+ 1 large ripe tomato
+ **2 cups** Silver Queen corn
+ 1 clove minced garlic
+ 1 hot pepper (optional)
+ **½ teaspoon** Old Bay seasoning
+ **½ teaspoon** cumin powder
+ Salt and pepper, to taste

Dice all vegetables ¼-inch square. In a medium skillet, lightly sauté onion and peppers in peanut oil. Add garlic, hot pepper, Old Bay, cumin, salt and pepper. Heat thoroughly, then spread out on a pan to cool. When cool, fold mixture in with tomato, zucchini, cucumber and corn.

Crab Hash

+ ½ **pound** lump crabmeat (picked through for shells)
+ 1 medium onion, diced
+ 2 large Idaho potatoes, peeled
+ 2 **tablespoons** butter
+ 1 **tablespoon** chopped fresh parsley
+ Salt and pepper, to taste

Boil potatoes until tender but not quite done in lightly salted water. Cool potatoes and cut into ¼-inch dice and set aside. Sauté onion until clear and shiny. Add potatoes, salt and pepper. Heat thoroughly; add crabmeat and parsley, again heating thoroughly. Remove from heat and serve.

Note: All preparations for crab hash can be done ahead and kept refrigerated except the addition of crab and parsley. This must be done right before serving.

Beurre Blanc

+ 4 shallots, sliced
+ 6 **ounces** white wine
+ 2 **tablespoons** heavy cream
+ 12 **ounces** unsalted butter (cut into pieces and room temperature)
+ Juice from 1 lemon
+ Salt, to taste

Heat shallots and white wine. Reduce until liquid is just about gone, then add cream. Bring cream to a boil and reduce by one half. Whisking constantly, slowly add butter, piece by piece, making sure sauce is not too hot. When all the butter has been added remove from heat, add lemon and salt to taste. Stir and strain. Keep warm until served using a warm water bath.

Blueberry Ketchup

For poultry dishes chef Henry liked to lighten things up with a sauce made from local fruit. A ketchup-type sauce, he served it with pan-fried chicken and grilled breast of duck.

Makes 12 servings

+ **1 pint** blueberries
+ **½ cup** honey cider vinegar (Bragg's makes a blend)
+ **4 tablespoons** brown sugar
+ **½ teaspoon** ground cinnamon
+ **¼ teaspoon** ground ginger
+ **¼ teaspoon** ground allspice
+ **¼ teaspoon** ground black pepper
+ **½ teaspoon** salt
+ **½ teaspoon** chopped garlic

Place all ingredients in a heavy-bottomed pot. Bring to a boil; reduce heat and simmer for 30 minutes. Strain through a fine sieve, cool and place in a plastic bottle with a fine tip. To serve, draw zigzags of sauce across sliced meat using the squeeze bottle. This sauce should be made a day in advance so the flavors can be fully developed.

Note: When serving with duck, Henry used wild blueberries for the sauce.

SPARKS, MD.

The
1740
MILTON
INN

CLOSE COVER BEFORE STRIKING

The Milton Inn's Cranberry Relish

This seasonal side dish is versatile and goes well with any type of poultry or game meats. It's a perfect dish to share on Thanksgiving Day.

Serves 8

+ 1 apple, diced
+ 1 pear, diced
+ **4 cups** fresh cranberries
+ 1 shallot, julienned
+ **1 cup** Earl Grey tea
+ **1 cup** granulated sugar
+ **1 cup** dark brown sugar
+ **¼ cup** whole butter
+ **¼ cup** honey
+ **1 teaspoon** vanilla extract

+ **¼ cup** brandy
+ 1 each juice and zest of orange and lime
+ **¼ teaspoon** salt
+ **¼ teaspoon** pepper
+ **¼ cup** candied ginger, julienned or small dice
+ **1 teaspoon** ground cinnamon
+ **1 teaspoon** ground star anise

Place all ingredients in a medium thick-bottomed pot. Bring to a boil and simmer over medium-low heat for 25 minutes. Bring to room temperature, refrigerate for at least 2 hours before serving.

My grandmother Geneva (on right) celebrates her birthday among family and friends in a private dining room at the Milton Inn, c. June 1991.

Chocolate Marble Terrine

This is a chocoholic's dream dessert, but consider yourself warned, it is time-consuming and expensive. The terrine is flourless and no-bake, making it ideal for summer.

Serves 8

+ **1 ½ pounds** bittersweet chocolate, such as Callebaut, chopped fine
+ **3 cups** heavy whipping cream
+ **2 pounds** white chocolate, such as Lindt Swiss White Chocolate

+ **2 cups** heavy whipping cream
+ **1 ½ pints** *Crème Anglaise*, (recipe follows) optional
+ Shelled, whole pistachio nuts or candied violets for garnish, optional

Bring 3 cups cream to boil in a two-quart saucepan. Remove from heat and allow to cool for 20 minutes. Skim the surface of the cream and pour into a double boiler set over medium heat. Do not allow the water to reach a boil.

Gradually add bittersweet chocolate to cream, stirring constantly with rubber spatula until all chocolate is melted and incorporated. Pour the ganache into a small stainless steel bowl and cover with plastic wrap to prevent a skin from developing. Allow to cool. Repeat process with the white chocolate.

Note: Both chocolate mixtures should cool to the point where they can be molded easily. If they are too soft, they will run into each other and the marbling effect will be lost. If the chocolates are too hard, they will not "marbleize" and will not pack neatly into the loaf pan.

To mold terrine: Grease a loaf pan and line it well with plastic wrap. In a mixing bowl, pour one ganache in first and then the second on top. Swirl a knife blade through the combined ganache's 3 or 4 times only. Too many swirls will cause the dark chocolate to dominate the white chocolate and the "marbleized" effect will be lost.

Pour into loaf pan. Cover filled pan with plastic wrap and freeze overnight.

To unmold terrine: Place pan in a little hot water to loosen. Do not leave in hot water for any longer than 30 seconds. Unmold and remove plastic wrap. Wrap it again and freeze for a couple hours or until hard.

☞

Crème Anglaise

+ **8** egg yolks

+ **6 ounces** granulated sugar

+ **1 cup** milk

+ **1 cup** heavy cream

+ **¼ teaspoon** vanilla extract

Place milk and cream in a large saucepan and bring to a boil. Remove from heat. In a mixing bowl, place yolks and sugar and whip until color lightens. Take 1/3 of boiled milk and cream; add to egg mixture.

Place remaining boiled milk, cream and egg mixture in double boiler over medium heat. Don't allow water to boil or your yolks will curdle. Stir constantly with rubber spatula until thick, about 20 minutes. Add vanilla extract.

To serve: Pour about 1 to 2 ounces of the Crème Anglaise on the plate. Center a ¼-inch thick slice of the terrine onto plate. Garnish with whole pistachio nuts or candied violets.

Raspberries with Lemon Curd in Meringue Shells

A sweet and tart winner on all counts! The lemon curd has incredible flavor and is elegant and easy to make ahead of time. It's a perfect summertime dessert and can be plated just before serving. Lemon curd can also be spooned over slices of pound cake or fresh berries if meringue shells are not available.

Serves 8

+ **3 half pints** fresh raspberries
+ **8** meringue shells, available in specialty stores
+ **4** large eggs, at room temperature
+ **½ to 2/3 cup** sugar, depending on your sweet tooth

+ **2** lemons, juice and zest, at room temperature
+ **5 tablespoons** unsalted butter at room temperature

For the lemon curd: Place about an inch of water in the bottom of a double boiler and bring to a boil. Turn down heat and keep warm until you are ready to cook. Whisk eggs, sugar, lemon juice and zest until well mixed. Place in the top of the double boiler over medium-low heat, stirring constantly with a wooden spoon (do not use a whisk).

Continue cooking until the mixture resembles a thick pudding and coats the back of a spoon. Be patient: thickening will take about 20 minutes. Then whisk in the butter. Pour the lemon curd into a glass lasagna pan or other flat pan and allow to cool for 10 minutes. Cover with plastic wrap and refrigerate until chilled. When cold, transfer to a storage container with a fitted lid.

Presentation: Place meringue shell in center of plate. Fill with approximately 2 tablespoons lemon curd. Arrange berries inside the lemon curd and scatter several about the plate.

Note: The Milton Inn kitchen prepared their own meringue shells, but since this is a summer dessert and humidity can easily ruin attempts at homemade meringue, chef Henry recommended purchasing the shells. The lemon curd is quite rich and if you don't have a sweet tooth, reduce the sugar to ½ cup.

Rudys' 2900

Neighborhood: Finksburg

2900 Baltimore Boulevard

Open: 1 9 8 3 - 2 0 0 5

Rudys' 2900, one of the most acclaimed fine dining institutions in the Baltimore area, was the success story and creation of two German-born Rudys: Rudolf "Rudi" Paul and Rudolph "Rudy" Speckamp. It was the epitome of outstanding European cooking and Maryland hospitality.

Both Rudys were chefs. Paul had apprenticed in his native East Germany before escaping to freedom in 1963. He practiced his trade in Europe before joining the historic Hamilton Princess in Bermuda. In 1975, Paul became the Maître d'hôtel of Peerce's Plantation in Baltimore County, which is how my family first became acquainted with him. Speckamp began work as a child apprentice in a hotel kitchen in his native Bavaria. One of this area's most visible chefs, he made his reputation at Samuel Owings 1767, a restaurant in Owings Mills and was later co-owner/chef at Capriccio in Little Italy. They were frequently mistaken for each other, which led Speckamp to phone Paul and suggest a meeting. They wound up becoming the best of friends and in 1983 the two men opened Rudys' 2900, named for the address of their Carroll County location on Route 140.

Paul, the consummate Maître d', oversaw the front of the house taking great care in visiting every table and inquiring as to each diner's pleasure. The kitchen was under the direction of Speckamp, who had earned his certified master chef (CMC) designation in 1988 from The American Culinary Federation - the industry's version of a medical degree. He was one of only 30 CMC's in the United States that year. As of 2019, there were only 66 CMC's in the country. It should also be noted that Speckamp was a gold-medal winner at the Culinary Olympics (1988) held in Frankfurt.

Rudys' menu offered continental cuisine with a Teutonic accent of classic dishes of game and seafood, often prepared with chef Speckamp's sophisticated sauces and reductions. In addition to the menu offerings, your server would recite a long list of specials, highlighted with fresh seasonal ingredients. Rudys' was not trendy. It leaned to the old-fashioned, catering to those who preferred continental cuisine over cutting edge. A careful balance of down home comfort and haute cuisine was just what their affluent and mature customers wanted.

The restaurant was quite pretty, resembling a comfortable European country inn. It had been decorated by Paul's talented wife, Rose. She chose a soothing palette of salmon and green floral wallpapers that nicely accented the mahogany-stained wood. Tables were widely spaced, covered with white linen, and set with fresh flowers, while comfortable banquettes were available for smaller parties. Staff were courteous and extremely knowledgeable. They would go out of their way to ensure a superb experience. Rudys' hosted unique culinary events like the annual Dinner with the Masters, where a half-dozen or so master chefs from around the country assembled at the restaurant, each preparing one course of the dinner. In 1999, seven visiting CMC's joined chef Speckamp in offering a seven-course dinner that included a champagne reception with hors d'oeuvres, appetizer, game birds, seafood, meat, salad, a palate cleansing sorbet, dessert and chocolate confections. It became an extremely popular annual event.

Hands down, Rudys' was my father's favorite restaurant and we often dined there over the years, celebrating birthdays and anniversaries. He and his wife Aliceann enjoyed hosting larger, private parties in their downstairs banquet room too. I remember my first visit to the restaurant. I had no idea where Finksburg was, but my father played chauffeur, and the journey was part of the charm. Setting off from his home in Lutherville we drove across bucolic Worthington Valley, all the while drinking in the sights of the "Horses and Hounds" scenic byway. As we approached the Finksburg building, its exterior did not look like much, but once inside it provided a contemporary provincial country setting, pretty and cozy. Rudi Paul was on hand to greet us. My father had a tremendous appreciation for Rudys' Old World finesse, with its gracious and attentive service and award-winning cuisine.

Countless awards were bestowed upon the restaurant including Restaurateurs of the Year (1989) by the Restaurant Association of Maryland, and the Achievement in Culinary Excellence Award presented by The American Culinary Federation in 2002. Rudys' 2900 was among six restaurants from around the country given the prize and the only one in the mid-Atlantic region.

It came as quite a blow to its loyal following in 2005 when the announcement came that Rudys' was closing. These two gentlemen will be remembered for their major contributions to Baltimore's reputation as a culinary destination.

Salmon Tartare

No cooking here, so it is best to select the freshest and best quality ingredients. This can be served as a light appetizer with toast triangles or as a brunch staple.

Serves 4 to 6

+ **1 pound** fresh salmon, bones and skin removed

+ **1** egg yolk

+ **2 tablespoons** Dijon mustard

+ **1 ½ cups** vegetable oil

+ ½ medium onion, finely diced

+ **1 tablespoon** capers

+ **4** anchovy filets, finely chopped

+ **1 ½ tablespoons** of fresh herbs, preferably dill or tarragon

Chop salmon in a food processor and set aside. In a large bowl, place egg yolk, mustard and vegetable oil. Whisk together until it forms an emulsion. Add in onion, capers, anchovies and fresh herbs, mixing to combine. Add the salmon and mix well.

Chef Rudy Speckamp introduces the seven nationally certified master chefs who have prepared the evenings seven-course dinner for 157 guests.

Maryland Crabmeat Gumbo

Patrick Dobbs, a young sous chef at Rudys' in 1988, represented his home state in the second annual American Seafood Challenge. This is the dish that put him in the Maryland finals.

Serves 6 to 8

+ **½ cup** chopped onion
+ **½ cup** chopped celery
+ **½ cup** chopped leeks
+ **½ cup** chopped green pepper
+ **3 to 4 tablespoons** vegetable oil
+ **1 teaspoon** chopped garlic
+ White and cayenne pepper, to taste
+ **1 teaspoon** seafood seasoning
+ **1 to 2 teaspoons** basil
+ **1 teaspoon** thyme
+ **1 to 2 teaspoons** oregano
+ **¼ cup** flour
+ **1 ½ quarts** fish stock (or clam juice)
+ **½ cup** diced tomatoes (blanched, peeled and diced; save juice)
+ **½ cup** okra
+ **2 tablespoons** gumbo filé (aka filé powder)
+ **½ to 1 pound** lump crabmeat
+ 12 fresh clams
+ 12 fresh oysters
+ **½ pound** shrimp
+ Cooked rice

Heat oil in a large pot or Dutch oven. Sauté onions, celery, leeks and green pepper until soft. Add garlic, cayenne and white pepper, seafood seasoning, basil, thyme and oregano. Stir to combine. Sprinkle flour over sautéed vegetables and stir well. Add fish stock and bring to a boil. Lower heat and simmer for 10 minutes.

Add okra and tomatoes, including tomato juices. Bring to a boil, lower heat and simmer for 30 minutes. Add gumbo filé, crabmeat, clams, oysters and shrimp, including any liquid. Simmer another 5 minutes. Serve with cooked rice, either as a bed at the bottom of soup bowl or on top of gumbo.

Pumpkin Bisque with Crisp Ginger

A bowl of this velvety bisque will hit the spot in the autumn and winter months. The addition of chili pepper and ginger offers a nice little zing that does not detract.

Serves 4 to 6

+ **1 tablespoon** diced onion
+ **1 cup** diced celery
+ **2** cloves chopped garlic
+ **1** minced, seedless chili pepper
+ **1 tablespoon** minced ginger
+ **4 cups** diced pumpkin
+ **4 cups** chicken stock
+ **2 cups** heavy cream

+ **½ cup** dark rum
+ **1 tablespoon** ground cumin
+ **1 teaspoon** ground coriander
+ **½ teaspoon** ground allspice
+ **½ teaspoon** salt
+ **½ teaspoon** white pepper
+ **½ cup** ginger, julienned
+ **1 cup** clarified butter

Heat oil in a large pot or Dutch oven. Add onion, celery, garlic, chili pepper and ginger. Sauté until vegetables are translucent. Add pumpkin and chicken stock. Bring to a boil, reduce heat and simmer for 40 to 45 minutes. Add cream, rum and seasonings.

Transfer soup to a food processor and blend until smooth. This can also be done using an immersion blender. Keep soup warm.

Heat clarified butter and add julienned ginger. Cook until crisp and golden brown. Before serving, sprinkle ginger over soup.

Seafood Sanibel

Ripe cantaloupe has a pleasing floral aroma and pairs so well with citrus and seafood. This refreshing summer salad can be tossed together in a snap and makes such an appealing presentation. Think tropic summer breezes and sandy white beaches!

Serves 4

+ 2 small cantaloupes
+ **4 ounces** lump crabmeat
+ **4 ounces** shrimp (21-25 count)
+ **4 ounces** scallops with roe
+ 2 oranges

Dressing:

+ **4 tablespoons** mayonnaise
+ **2 tablespoons** chili sauce

+ **1 teaspoon** horseradish
+ **1 teaspoon** fresh chopped tarragon
+ **1 tablespoon** orange juice
+ **1 tablespoon** pineapple juice
+ **1 teaspoon** brandy
+ Worcestershire sauce, to taste
+ **½ cup** whipped cream

Peel cantaloupes, cut in half diagonally, remove pulp, and set aside. Cook shrimp and scallops just until tender, and chill. Peel and cut oranges into sections. Except for whipped cream, mix all dressing ingredients until smooth. Fold in whipped cream.

Toss seafood and orange sections with the dressing. To serve, place in chilled cantaloupe halves and garnish with tarragon or mint leaves.

Rudys' 2900 presents Dinner with the Masters to celebrate the restaurants' 16th anniversary on September 13, 1999.

Seared Rockfish with Oyster and Corn Stew

Rich Hoffman of Rudys' 2900 entered this dish in The Maryland Rockfish Celebration Cooking Contest (2003) sponsored by the Maryland Department of Agriculture's Seafood Marketing Program. He walked off with the first-place prize.

Serves 4

Oyster and Corn Stew:

+ **4 ounces** (1 stick) butter
+ **1 pint** half-and-half
+ **1 tablespoon** chopped red bell pepper
+ **¼ cup** each diced celery, onions, shallots and leeks
+ **¼ cup** diced wild mushrooms, freshest possible
+ **2 ounces** dry Vermouth
+ **1 tablespoon** finely chopped parsley, tarragon, basil
+ **¼ cup** coarsely chopped, peeled tomatoes
+ Salt and pepper
+ **8 ounces** oyster liquor
+ **12** large plump Maryland oysters
+ **2 tablespoons** flour
+ **1 cup** roasted corn

Heat butter in a stock pot. Add celery, onions, shallots, leeks, mushrooms, red bell pepper and roasted corn. Sauté until vegetables are tender. Add flour to make a blonde roux. Deglaze with the Vermouth and cook out the alcohol. Add the oyster liquor and half-and-half. Simmer for 25 minutes over low heat until the roux is thickened. It should coat the back of a spoon. Season to taste with salt and pepper. Remove from the heat and add the oysters, tomatoes and chopped herbs. Serve with hot fillets.

Seared Rockfish:

+ **2 pounds** rockfish filets (cut into four 6-ounce portions)
+ Clarified butter
+ Ground mustard seed
+ Salt
+ Cracked black pepper
+ Lemon juice

Preheat oven to 350°F. Season the fish with salt, pepper and mustard seed. In a sauté pan, heat the clarified butter. Sear the fish until golden brown on both sides. Place in oven for about 8 minutes or until done. Sprinkle the fish with lemon juice and serve hot.

Grouper and Salmon in Orange and Fennel Butter

Serves 4

+ **16 ounces** boneless grouper filet
+ **16 ounces** boneless salmon filet
+ 1 fennel (separate sprigs from stalk and save 4 nice sprigs for garnish, chop the rest of the sprigs, cut stalk very thin in bias juliennes and divide in half)
+ 1 orange, cut in skinless and seedless sections
+ ½ **cup** fish stock
+ ½ **cup** white wine (if fish stock is not available, use all white wine)
+ **1 cup** orange juice
+ **1 cup** heavy cream
+ **8 ounces** (2 sticks) butter
+ 2 shallots, chopped
+ Salt and pepper to taste

Cut each fish into 2-ounce slices. Place on a buttered sheet pan - fan out 4 portions alternating the grouper and salmon filets. Set aside.

In a large saucepan, simmer fish stock, white wine, orange juice, shallots and half of the fennel juliennes until the fennel is cooked and the liquid reduced until almost dry. Put in food processor, blend until smooth, and return to pot. Add cream. Reduce until cream thickens. Whip in butter a little at a time. Add some of the chopped fennel sprigs, salt and pepper to taste. Keep warm in a double boiler.

Place sheet pan under hot broiler for 3 to 4 minutes or until done. Sauté the remainder of the fennel juliennes in butter (al dente). Season with salt, pepper and chopped fennel sprigs. Add orange sections.

Place sauce on bottom of 4 warm plates. Carefully add broiled fish slices (2 salmon and 2 grouper each). Top with sautéed fennel juliennes and orange sections. Garnish with fennel sprigs.

Soft Shell Crabs with Corn Relish, Field Greens and Roasted Red Pepper Sauce

The Great American Seafood Cook-Off is an annual competition; 15 chefs from 14 states prepared their best dishes using seafood indigenous to their state. Chef Rudy was handpicked by Governor Robert Ehrlich to represent Maryland. He won the bronze medal for this crab dish. The episode can still be viewed on Food Network Challenge.

Serves 4

+ **1 quart** peanut oil
+ **8 ounces** all-purpose flour
+ **2 ounces** cornstarch
+ **¼ teaspoon** freshly ground black pepper
+ **¼ teaspoon** ground fennel
+ **½ teaspoon** salt
+ **1 cup** club soda

+ **4** egg whites, beaten until frothy
+ **8** small soft shell crabs, cleaned
+ ***Corn Relish***, recipe follows
+ ***Roasted Red Pepper Sauce***, recipe follows
+ **2 cups** mixed field greens, for garnish

In a deep saucepan, heat peanut oil to 350°F. In a large bowl, whisk together flour, cornstarch, pepper, fennel and salt. Whisk in club soda and egg whites to form a smooth batter. Dip soft shells in batter and fry in batches until golden brown, about 4 minutes. Drain on paper towels.

Corn Relish:

+ **2** ears corn, husked and silk removed
+ **2 tablespoons** olive oil
+ **3 ounces** asparagus, sliced into ½" pieces
+ **4 ounces** mushrooms, sliced
+ **¼ cup** diced red bell pepper
+ **1** small jalapeno, diced, without seeds

+ **1** green onion, thinly sliced
+ **2 tablespoons** light brown sugar
+ **3 tablespoons** cider vinegar
+ **½ tablespoon** dry mustard
+ Dash hot pepper sauce
+ **1 teaspoon** Worcestershire sauce
+ **½ teaspoon** salt

Steam corn kernels until crisp-tender, about 3 to 5 minutes. Set aside. Cut the kernels of the cob into a mixing bowl.

In a large skillet, heat olive oil over medium-high heat. Add asparagus and mushrooms. Cook until mushrooms give off liquid and begin to brown, about 3 to 5 minutes. Add red bell pepper, jalapeno, and green onion. Cook just until green onion wilts, about 2 minutes. Add remaining ingredients and bring to a boil. Stir in corn mixture and cook until corn is heated through.

Roasted Red Pepper Sauce:

+ ½ **cup** roasted red pepper puree
+ **4** shallots, diced
+ **4 ounces** cider vinegar
+ ¼ **cup** heavy cream
+ **2 ounces** lemon juice
+ **8 ounces** unsalted butter, cubed
+ Salt to taste

Combine pepper puree, shallots and cider vinegar in a non-reactive saucepan. Bring to boil and simmer gently until shallots are tender. Add cream and stir to combine. Add lemon juice and whisk in butter, one piece at a time until sauce is smooth and thickened. Season with salt to taste. Serve crabs with *Corn Relish*, drizzle with *Roasted Red Pepper Sauce* and garnish each serving with a handful of greens.

Lobster Gratin with Green and White Asparagus

Chef Rudy offered cooking classes at the restaurant periodically. He generously shared this extravagant and indulgent recipe modified for home preparation.

Serves 8

+ **Four 1 ½ pound** lobsters
+ **24** green asparagus spears, blanched
+ **24** white asparagus spears, blanched

Sauce:

+ **1** lobster shell
+ **¼ cup** mirepoix (finely chopped celery, onion, carrot)
+ **1 ½ tablespoons** tomato paste
+ **2 tablespoons** brandy

+ **¼ cup** white wine
+ **¼ cup** red wine
+ **1** bay leaf
+ **½ teaspoon** caraway seeds
+ **½ teaspoon** fennel seeds
+ **1/8 teaspoon** cracked black pepper
+ **2 cups** fish stock
+ Cornstarch
+ **½ tablespoon** butter

Bring a stock pot of water to a boil. Add lobsters and cook until done, about 8 minutes. Drain and chill. Extract lobster meat from the shells and chill. Reserve 1 shell.

In a hot pan, roast lobster shell until evenly browned. Add mirepoix and continue to cook, stirring frequently until color develops. stir in tomato paste and pan roast until aroma develops. Deglaze with brandy and wines.

Add bay leaf, caraway, fennel, and pepper. Reduce until dry. Add fish stock and gently simmer until reduced by half. Strain through a fine sieve. Finish the sauce with the addition of cornstarch. Just before serving, gradually stir in butter and remove bay leaf.

Glacage:

+ **2** egg yolks
+ **¼ cup** heavy cream, whipped

Mix ½ cup lobster sauce with egg yolks. Stir in whipped cream. On ovenproof plates, arrange lobster meat and asparagus. Pour ¼ cup of lobster sauce over each portion, then top with 2 tablespoons of *glacage*. Place under the broiler until *glacage* is lightly browned.

Boneless Breast of Pheasant stuffed with Game Sausage in Apple Brandy Sauce

This signature dish was served Bavarian style with a side of red cabbage and homemade spaetzle, but sautéed apples would be a delicious accompaniment too.

Serves 4

- + 2 pheasants
- + **3-4 ounces** fat back, cut into chunks and frozen
- + **1 teaspoon** mustard seed
- + **¼ teaspoon** garlic powder
- + Salt and pepper, to taste
- + **1 ½ teaspoons** marjoram

- + **4** sausage casings
- + **2-3 tablespoons** butter
- + **1 ½ ounces** apple brandy
- + **1/3 cup** pheasant stock (made from bones of the pheasant)
- + **1/3 cup** heavy cream
- + Sausage casings

Separate the legs from the breasts and debone all. Mince the leg meat in a food processor. Add the frozen fat back, mustard seed, garlic powder, salt, pepper and marjoram. Pipe this mixture into sausage casings. Bake or grill until golden brown and firm to the touch. Keep warm in low oven.

Heat butter in a skillet until extremely hot; brown the breasts on both sides until one-quarter done. Remove the breasts and place in the oven to keep warm. In the same skillet, add the apple brandy, pheasant stock and heavy cream. Reduce until the desired consistency and adjust seasonings. Return breasts to sauce and gently simmer for another 1 to 2 minutes or until completely cooked.

To serve, place breasts and sauce on a plate. Thinly slice the sausages and fan the slices out on the plate next to the breasts.

Fettuccine Carbonara

Serves 4 to 6

+ **8 ounces** bacon, pancetta or Tasso ham, cut in small cubes

+ **1 pound** fettuccine

+ **4** eggs

+ **2 cups** heavy cream

+ **1 tablespoon** cracked black pepper

+ **4 tablespoons** grated Parmesan or Romano cheese

+ **1 tablespoon** chopped parsley

In a large skillet, sauté the bacon until crisp. Meanwhile cook the fettuccine noodles in rapidly boiling water to al dente. Drain noodles and add to the crisp bacon.

In a bowl, whisk together eggs, cream, peppercorns, cheese and parsley. Pour over hot fettuccine and bacon. Toss well and serve immediately.

Co-host Rudi Paul.

Roasted Parsnip Puree

My dad loved his parsnips, and no one whipped them up better than chef Rudy.

Serves 8 to 10

+ **8 ounces** russet potatoes, peeled
+ **2 ounces** unsalted butter
+ **1 cup** vegetable stock
+ **1/8 teaspoon** white pepper
+ **2 pounds** parsnips, peeled
+ **½ pound** onions, sliced
+ **½ teaspoon** salt

Preheat oven to 375°F. In a steamer basket, steam potatoes until soft and puree. Set aside.

Steam the parsnips until slightly softened. In a shallow oven proof sauté pan, sweat the onions in the butter. Add the stock, salt and pepper and bring to a boil. Add the parsnips and toss to distribute with the onions. Place in oven, occasionally tossing and basting the parsnips in the reducing stock until they are tender, and the stock is reduced to a glaze.

Puree the parsnips and onions, combine with the potato puree and strain. Adjust the seasoning with salt and pepper as needed.

Raspberries Romanoff

The name alone evokes a vision of a majestic dessert. It became all the rage in America during the late '40s when "Prince" Mike Romanoff introduced the signature dish at his namesake Beverly Hills restaurant. This simple dessert is a great way to serve a refreshing parfait that can be easily prepared between courses.

Serves 4

+ **2 ½ pints** ripe raspberries
+ **1 cup** vanilla ice cream, softened
+ **2 ounces** Port wine
+ **1 ounce** Grand Marnier or other orange flavored liqueur

+ **½ cup** Melba sauce (use a commercial brand)
+ **1 cup** heavy cream

Divide 2 pints raspberries among 4 stemmed Champagne coupe glasses. Chill. Purée the remaining ½ pint of raspberries and stir into softened ice cream. Add Port, Grand Marnier and Melba sauce, stirring gently until well blended.

Beat heavy cream until lightly whipped (it should form soft peaks). Gently fold into the ice cream mixture. Pour over raspberries and serve.

With attention to detail, chef Rudy and sous chef place garnishes purposefully as they ready plates for the next course.

Pecan Diamonds

Makes about 200 cookies

Cookie dough:

+ **10 tablespoons** butter, softened
+ **9 tablespoons** sugar
+ **6 tablespoons** solid shortening
+ **1** egg
+ **½ teaspoon** vanilla extract
+ **3 cups** all-purpose flour
+ **1 teaspoon** baking powder
+ **½ teaspoon** salt
+ **Filling:**
+ **2 cups** butter (**1 pound**)
+ **1 1/8 cups** honey
+ **½ cup** granulated sugar
+ **2 ½ cups** light brown sugar (**1 pound**)
+ **8 cups** chopped pecans or walnuts
+ **½ cup** heavy cream

Preheat oven to 375°F. To make the cookie dough, cream together butter, sugar and shortening until smooth. Add the egg and vanilla extract. In a separate bowl, sift together flour, baking powder and salt. Add to the creamed ingredients and mix to a smooth dough. Wrap and refrigerate overnight.

Using a floured cloth, roll out the dough to a 12x16-inch rectangle, 1 inch thick. Invert the dough onto a 12x16-inch baking sheet and prick all over with a fork. Partially bake the dough in the preheated oven for about 10 minutes. DO NOT BROWN. Allow the dough to cool while you make the filling.

Lower oven temperature to 350°F. Combine butter, honey, and sugars in a large saucepan over medium heat. Bring to a boil and boil for exactly 3 minutes. Remove from the heat and fold in the nuts and then the heavy cream. DO NOT STIR. Spread immediately over the partially baked crust. Double pan and bake in a preheated 350°F oven for 35 minutes. Cool completely and cut into small diamonds to serve.

PART THREE: THE CRAB COOKING OLYMPICS

East - West Crab Fight

In the days that followed the death of former Baltimore mayor, Tommy D'Alesandro III in October of 2019, I listened to news reports and read articles about his leadership, and his many political accomplishments. Something I was not reading about, that I had only recently discovered while doing research for this book, was another of his enormous contributions to the city of Baltimore. It was inspired by a comment he once made when talking shop with fellow Mayor Joseph Alioto of San Francisco. There's no doubt that his remark helped to put the city in the national spotlight and went a long way toward establishing Baltimore as a major culinary destination.

Do you recall when Baltimore participated in the 1969 Crab Cooking Olympics in San Francisco? I had been completely unaware of it, but this crustacean cook-off was a big deal. As the story goes, the cook-off was a direct result of an exchange between Mayor D'Alesandro and Mayor Alioto. D'Alesandro was quoted as saying that Chesapeake Bay crabs were "supreme to any other in the universe," including the Dungeness crabs of the west. This incited a coast-to-coast debate about whose crabs were better. Obviously fired up, Mayor Alioto challenged Mayor D'Alesandro to prove that Baltimore was the best at cooking crabs. The fight took the form of a culinary competition masterminded by famed chef and author, James Beard. Beard was among a distinguished panel of food experts serving as judges.

Though the idea started out as a friendly two-city competition, from coast-to-coast other professional chefs jumped on the bandwagon. The first annual Crab Cooking Olympics was officially kicked off in May of 1969. Dave Gordon, owner of Gordon's of Orleans Street, would represent Baltimore and compete against 16 other crab chef professionals from 17 cities. The contestants were vying for the ultimate title, "Maître Chef de Cuisine," and they competed in five categories: Crab au Gratin, Crab Cioppino or Bouillabaisse, Deviled Crab, Crab Louis, and a specialty of their choice. Each dish was judged on the basis of its appearance, taste, presentation, and originality. In subsequent years, there were slight variations on these five categories.

Dave Gordon's Baltimore-style crab cakes won the chef's first place specialty prize and he was advised in advance by Mayor D'Alesandro to "accept your inevitable award for our obviously superior crab cakes with the traditional modesty becoming of a Baltimorean." Unfortunately for Baltimore, the top honor went to a San Francisco chef. But take heart, before the contest even got off the ground, some observers were calling it rigged in favor of Dungeness. Atlantic blue crab is not normally used in dishes like Crab Louis or Cioppino, as both dishes had been invented to glorify Pacific crab. The competition was held twice more, in 1970 and 1971, then following a nine-year hiatus it was revived again in 1980. It was finally held in Baltimore at the historic Lexington Market in 1982. As to which crab is better, West or East, in 1982 that question remained unanswered according to the Baltimore *Evening Sun*. But *we* know.

I thought it would be fun to close out this book with a collection of the Olympic crab dish recipes entered by the chefs that represented Baltimore across all the annual competitions. While some dishes won coveted awards and others did not, to me they are all winners - these are the dishes that our chefs were most proud of, and they symbolize the excellence of Baltimore blue crab cookery.

Gordon's of Orleans Street

Owner/chef: Dave Gordon

Category: Chef's Specialty

Prize awarded: First Place (1969)

Maryland Crab Cakes

Dave Gordon reported back from San Francisco that his Baltimore-style crab cakes were hailed as "The best I've ever eaten," by the most celebrated judge, author, and cook, James Beard.

Makes 4 crab cakes

+ **1 pound** backfin lump Maryland crab
+ **¼ cup** dry breadcrumbs
+ **¼ cup** mayonnaise
+ **¼ cup** white sauce
+ **2** eggs
+ **1 teaspoon** white pepper
+ **1 teaspoon** salt
+ Oil for frying or butter

In a large bowl, mix crabmeat and breadcrumbs. In another bowl mix mayonnaise, white sauce and eggs. Add wet mixture to crabmeat and breadcrumbs, mixing thoroughly.

Shape into patties approximately 4 ounces each. Fry in deep fat (pure vegetable oil) at 350°F for about 3 minutes. Alternately, place on a greased broiler pan, brush with melted butter and broil until golden brown.

Serve two crab cakes per person with tartar sauce, French fries and coleslaw.

Thompson's Sea Girt House

Owner/chef: George W. "Tommy" Thompson, Jr.

Category: Crab Imperial

Imperial Crab á la Maryland

Among Thompson's entries was this original family recipe for crab imperial created at the restaurant in the late 19th century. About a week before the competition he demonstrated his preparation of the dish for a group of seafood promoters and Maryland seafood lovers at the restaurant. Chef Thompson advised the audience to handle the meat very delicately, and he emphasized the importance of not making the mixture too wet, so that the mounded backfin could be formed into cone shapes that would stay intact. It was quite an upset for Baltimore when the dish failed to bring home a top prize!

Serves 4

+ 1 egg, beaten
+ **2 tablespoons** mayonnaise
+ **1 pound** of fresh lump crabmeat
+ Chopped green peppers, to taste
+ Chopped pimentos, to taste
+ **1 teaspoon** melted butter

+ **1 teaspoon** salt
+ **2 teaspoons** Worcestershire sauce
+ **¼ teaspoon** red pepper
+ **¼ teaspoon** green pepper
+ **¼ teaspoon** white pepper

Preheat oven to 350° for 10 minutes.

Mix all ingredients except crabmeat together until well blended. Very gently add the crab lumps to the mayonnaise mixture and toss to coat. Mold crabmeat mixture into 4-inch cones and place in 4 crabmeat shells on a baking sheet. Bake for about 20 minutes or until outside of cones become golden brown.

Note: Although Mr. Thompson demonstrated the dish using chopped green peppers and pimentos, no specific amounts were given. As he molded the mixture into 4-inch cones he said, "the secret of keeping it firm was not to overcook it." When presented at the restaurant the dish was topped with an American flag toothpick.

Angelina's

Owner/chef: Robert "Bob" Reilly

Category:

Prize awarded: "most artistic" (1980)

Maryland Crab Cakes

I included Angelina's crab cake recipe in my first book, Dining Down Memory Lane. I later found this recipe submitted by chef Bob Reilly to the San Francisco Examiner during the 1980 Crab Cooking Olympics. For me, this one rings truer as I recall the crab cakes at Angelina's being much larger than the other recipe. Chef Reilly told the Examiner that there were three secrets: use fresh white bread crumbs rather than dry which keeps the texture soft, handle the crabmeat as little as possible to keep the lumps intact, and brown the crab cakes just enough to heat them through as the meat is already cooked. He further added, "My feeling with crabmeat is that it's very delicate. If you put too many spices in, you can't taste the crab anymore. We use only fresh Chesapeake channel blue crabs." The judges did not get around to tasting them for two hours which would explain why he wasn't awarded top honors for the dish.

Makes 4*

+ **1 pound** lump crabmeat
+ **¼ teaspoon** salt
+ **¼ teaspoon** white pepper
+ **¼ teaspoon** monosodium glutamate (optional)
+ **1 tablespoon** chopped parsley
+ **2 slices** white bread, crusts removed
+ Milk, to moisten
+ **½ teaspoon** baking powder
+ **1** egg
+ **2 tablespoon** mayonnaise

In a mixing bowl, combine the crabmeat, salt, white pepper, MSG and parsley. Grind the bread to exceptionally fine crumbs in a food processor. Soak it in milk and squeeze dry. Add the crumbs to the crab.

Beat the egg, baking powder and mayonnaise to make a thick sauce. Mix this lightly with the crab and form the mixture into four balls. Let them stand for at least ½ an hour.

To deep-fry (restaurant style): Heat the oil to 375°F. Lower the crab cakes into the oil and fry for no more than 5 minutes, just long enough to brown. Drain them on paper towels.

To pan-fry (home style): Pour vegetable oil in a large frying pan to a depth of ½-inch. Flatten the balls somewhat, and brown them lightly in hot oil. Drain them on paper towels.

*According to the *Evening Sun*, Reilly made baseball-sized cakes and got only three per pound.

Chef: Robert Reilly

Category: Crab Cioppino

Prize awarded: First Place: (1982) Baltimore

Third Place: (1982) San Francisco

Crab Cioppino

A fish stew associated with San Francisco and believed to have originated with its Italian immigrants. Serve with plenty of crusty bread to soak up the broth.

Serves 4

For the broth:

+ **3 tablespoons** olive oil
+ I medium onion, diced
+ **2 tablespoons** parsley, minced
+ **3 tablespoons** flour
+ **1 quart** tomato-clam juice
+ **1 pound** tomatoes, peeled, seeded and chopped
+ **1 ½ teaspoons** seafood seasoning
+ **1 teaspoon** salt
+ **½ teaspoon** black pepper

In a stockpot, sauté onion in olive oil until translucent. Stir in parsley. Blend in flour and slowly add tomato-clam juice, tomatoes and seasonings. Bring to a boil, then simmer for two hours. When the broth is developed, poach seafood in wine.

Seafood:

+ **1 pound** crabmeat
+ **1 pound** shrimp, peeled (leave tail on)
+ **½ pound** small scallops
+ **1 pound** firm white fish, fileted (cut in serving pieces)
+ 6 small clams, leave in shell
+ 6 black mussels, leave in shell
+ **1 pint** dry white wine
+ 1 bay leaf
+ Garlic croutons

Heat wine with bay leaf; poach seafood in order of time required to cook. Add crab meat last, just to heat. Remove bay leaf. Add seafood and poaching liquid to broth. Serve with garlic croutons.

Chef: Robert Reilly

Category: Crab Louis or Crab salad

Prize awarded: First place for most artistic (1980)

Crab Louis

This famous recipe was originated by the chef at the Olympic Club in Seattle, Washington. The story goes that Enrico Caruso of the Metropolitan Opera Company sang in the city in 1904 and could not get enough Crab Louis, eating so much that there was none left in the kitchen.

Serves 8

+ **2 pounds** crabmeat
+ **½ cup** celery, diced finely
+ **½ cup** sweet apple, diced
+ **½ cup** tomato, skinned, seeded and diced
+ **1 tablespoon** chopped parsley
+ **1 cup** crushed seafood-seasoned potato chips
+ **1** pickled egg, chopped
+ **½ teaspoon** white pepper
+ **1 teaspoon** salt

Toss all ingredients. Blend in Louis dressing, below.

Louis Dressing
+ **½ cup** mayonnaise
+ **½ cup** sour cream
+ **1 cup** chili sauce relish

Mix dressing lightly, blend into crab mixture. Mold or lay on lettuce rafts or a bed of shredded lettuce. Garnish with pickled egg wedges, tomatoes, whole seafood-seasoned potato chips and parsley.

Chef: Robert Reilly

Category: Deviled Crab

Prize awarded: First Place (1982)

Deviled Crab

(Spicy Imperial Crab)

Serves 8

For the broth:

+ **4 pounds** crabmeat
+ **2 tablespoons** dry mustard
+ **4 teaspoons** minced parsley
+ **1 teaspoon** salt
+ **2 tablespoons** Worcestershire sauce
+ **1 tablespoon** Old Bay seafood seasoning
+ **8** slices fresh breadcrumbs without crust
+ **8** drops Tabasco sauce

+ **12 tablespoons** mayonnaise
+ **4** fresh eggs
+ **4 tablespoons** pimiento, diced fine
+ **4 tablespoons** green pepper, parboiled, diced fine
+ **2 teaspoons** Hungarian paprika

For topping:

+ Fresh breadcrumbs
+ Clarified butter, as needed
+ Hungarian paprika

Preheat oven to 350°F. Place crabmeat in a bowl. In a small bowl, blend dry mustard, salt, Old Bay and paprika. Sprinkle dry seasonings over crabmeat. Add breadcrumbs, diced green pepper and pimiento. Beat eggs and mayonnaise lightly, add Worcestershire sauce and Tabasco, pour over breadcrumb mixture and toss gently. Mound in natural crab shells or ramekins. Top with fresh bread-crumb topping, drizzle with clarified butter on top and garnish with pimiento. Bake for 20 minutes.

Chef: Robert Reilly

Category: Chefs specialty (1982)

Crab Brendan

Reilly created and named this dish for his son and served it at his restaurant, Angelina's.

Serves 4

+ 4 medium tomatoes
+ 1 teaspoon seafood seasoning
+ 1 pound crabmeat
+ 2 tablespoons mayonnaise
+ 1 egg
+ ½ teaspoon white pepper
+ Crumbs from 2 slices fresh bread, crusts removed
+ ¼ teaspoon baking powder
+ 1 teaspoon minced parsley
+ ½ teaspoon salt
+ ½ teaspoon Hungarian paprika
+ 4 fresh shrimp

Preheat oven to 350°F. Place crabmeat in mixing bowl. add breadcrumbs. Sprinkle baking powder on crumbs and add salt, pepper and parsley. Beat egg with mayonnaise, pour over crab-breadcrumb mixture and toss lightly.

Cut tops off tomatoes and hollow out insides. Sprinkle inside walls of tomato with seafood seasoning. Distribute crabmeat mixture into each tomato, peak crabmeat, sprinkle with Hungarian paprika and place butterflied shrimp on top. Bake on buttered shells for 20 minutes.

Chef: Robert Reilly

Category: Nouvelle Cuisine (1982)

California Crab Cornets

Serves 8

+ **2 pounds** crabmeat
+ **4 ounces** unsalted butter
+ **½ cup** tomato, skinned, seeded and chopped
+ **2 teaspoons** chopped parsley
+ **2** black olives, chopped
+ **½ teaspoon** white pepper
+ **1 teaspoon** salt
+ **8** large lettuce leaves
+ *Cranberry Sauce*, recipe follows

Blanch the lettuce leaves, dry and set aside. Heat butter, and sauté crabmeat, tomato, parsley, black olives and seasonings. Cook about 5 minutes to blend and warm through. Remove from heat.

Divide mixture and place into lettuce leaves and roll filled leaves into horns. Trim open end so all cones are even. Put cranberry sauce in center of serving dish and arrange cones out from sauce in sunburst design. Garnish with tomatoes and olive slices.

Cranberry Sauce:

+ **8 ounces** cranberry juice
+ **2 ounces** rice vinegar
+ **2 ounces** dry white wine
+ **8 ounces** heavy cream
+ **1 pound** unsalted butter

Heat cranberry juice, rice vinegar and dry wine together and reduce to approximately 4 tablespoons. Add cream, heat, and reduce further. Whip in butter a little at a time.

Broadview Restaurant

Chef: Paul Bartlett

Category: Nouvelle Cuisine

Prize awarded: Second place (1983)

Crab Norfolk

Serves 8

+ **1 ounce** clarified butter
+ **3 pounds** backfin crabmeat, picked clean of shells
+ **3 ounces** country or prosciutto ham, julienned
+ **4** scallions without tops, julienned
+ **6 ounces** Madeira
+ Chopped parsley
+ **¼ pound** cold butter, cut in pieces
+ **8** parsley sprigs

Preheat oven to 350°F. Heat butter in a large ovenproof sauté pan. Drop in ham and scallions. Roll once. Add Madeira (Madeira should flame). If alcohol is not burned off in flame, allow Madeira to reduce for a minute. Add crabmeat.

Roll pan once. That is, bring the ham and scallions to the top. Sprinkle with chopped parsley and dot with cold butter. Place pan in hot oven for two minutes until butter melts and mixture is hot. Spoon carefully into 8 ramekins. Garnish with parsley sprigs.

Sources

RECIPES

The Bakery's

Doebereiner's Chocolate Cake - Rothman, Julie. "A Sweet Memory from an Old Baltimore Bakery." *Baltimore Sun* 11 May 2016: C2. Print. Adapted from a recipe contributed by Audrey Crooks (having received the recipe from her neighbor Peggy Sindall, daughter of George Doebereiner).

Hutzler's-Wellesley Cake - Kelly, Jacques. "Dining at Hutzler's was a Baltimore Tradition." *Baltimore Sun* 8 Nov 1989: D1+. Print. Adapted from a recipe contributed by Hannah Mazo, Hutzler's personnel manager.

Ms. Dessert's Chocolate Walnut Pastry and Chocolate Zucchini Cake - Goldbloom, Shelley. "Bakery founder offers recipes." *LaCrosse Tribune* 12 Apr 1983: 10. Print. Adapted from recipes contributed by Dean Kolstad, founder of the Baltimore bakery, Ms. Desserts

Rice's Louisiana Ring Cake - Roeder, Virginia. "Ring Cake Recipe Appeal Brings A Double Feature." *Evening Sun* (Baltimore) 10 Aug 1966: C3. Print. Adapted from a recipe contributed by Mrs. Albert Blankman.

Silber's Mandel Bread and Honey Cake - Roeder, Virginia. "Holiday Foods with a Baltimore flavor." *Baltimore Sun* 12 Dec 1971: 24-25. Print. Adapted from recipes contributed by Dora Silber.

The Restaurants

House of Winterling

Poor Man's Lobster - Adapted from D'Adamo, Joe. "Touches of class in a place like home." *Evening Sun* (Baltimore) 4 Sept 1980: 18. Print.

Swiss Steaks and Apple Crumb Pie - Canton Library Centennial Committee. *Canton Branch Cookbook: A Collection of Recipes from Neighbors, Staff, and Friends of the Canton Library*. Baltimore: Enoch Pratt free Library, 1986. Print.

Haussner's

Baked Herbed Oysters - Patterson, Suzanne. "Gourmet Holidays Baltimore." *Gourmet* Oct 1981: 32+. Print. Adapted from a recipe contributed by Haussner's Restaurant.

Tomato Florentine Soup - Rothman, Julie. "Just add a grilled cheese sandwich." *Baltimore Sun* 1 Feb 2012: C3. Print. Adapted from a recipe contributed by Nancy Cohen, owner of Eddie's of Roland Park.

Grilled Salmon Kabobs and Seasoned Lemon Rice - Adapted from Baker, Mary Lou, and Bonnie Rapoport Marshall. *Dining In - Baltimore Cookbook Vol. II* Seattle: Peanut Butter, 1988. Print.

Hasenpfeffer - Adapted from D'Adamo, Joe. "Haussner's poses a few riddles." *Evening Sun* (Baltimore) 22 Mar 1984: 44. Print.

Spaetzle, Hungarian Goulash and Potato Dumpling's - Patterson, Suzanne. "Gourmet Holidays Baltimore." *Gourmet* Oct 1981: 32+. Print. Adapted from recipes contributed by Haussner's Restaurant.

Tyrolean Dumplings - Adapted from Rapoport, Bonnie. *Dining In - Baltimore: A Collection of Gourmet Recipes for Complete Meals* Seattle: Peanut Butter, 1981. Print.

Oysters and Smithfield Ham á la Haussner's - Maryland Chapter Arthritis Foundation. *Beyond Beer & Crabs* Memphis: Wimmer Brothers, 1982. Print.

Paprika Schnitzel - Patterson, Suzanne. "Gourmet Holidays Baltimore." *Gourmet* Oct 1981: 32+. Print. Adapted from a recipe contributed by Haussner's Restaurant.

Roasted fresh ham with fruit and herb stuffing - Dorsey, John. "Food and Art: The hearty flavors of Frances Haussner's life." *Baltimore Sun* 16 Nov 1986: 1J+. Print. Adapted from a recipe contributed by Haussner's Restaurant.

Weiner Schnitzel - "R.S.V.P.," *Bon Appétit* Sept: 1999: 24+. Print. Adapted from a recipe contributed by Francie Haussner George, proprietor of Haussner's Restaurant.

Fried Eggplant - *Favorite Recipes from our Best Cooks Cookbook*. Baltimore: PTA Hillendale Elementary School, 1975-1976. Print. Adapted from a recipe contributed by Haussner's Restaurant.

Lemon Chiffon Cake and Strawberry Soup - Adapted from Fish, Kathleen DeVanna. *Cooking Secrets from Mid-Atlantic and Chesapeake*. Monterey: Bon Vivant 2000. Print.

Maria's "300"

Garlic Bread - H., Joe. "Garlic Bread...To Die For!" *Chowhound* Home Cooking Forum, 22 Dec 2007. www.chowhound.com/post/garlic-breadto-die-471992?commentld=4589469

Braciola - Dempsey, Margaret. "Thought for Food." *Evening Sun* (Baltimore) 23 Jun 1949: 20. Print. Adapted from a recipe contributed by Maria Allori, proprietor of Maria's "300".

Capriccio

Toast Capriccio - *The Baltimore All-America City "Star Spangled" Cookbook*. Guilford Cookbook Committee, Baltimore: 1977. Print. Adapted from a recipe contributed by owner/chef Rudy Speckamp.

Rigatoni alla Vodka, Scampi Capriccio, Chicken Gismonda, Veal Scallops with Mozzarella and Prosciutto and Strawberry Zabaglione - Patterson, Suzanne. "Gourmet Holidays Baltimore." *Gourmet* Oct 1981: 32+. Print. Adapted from recipes contributed to by Capriccio Restaurant.

Miller Brothers

Southern Chicken a la Maryland - *Parade*. "Southern Fried Chicken." *Detroit Free Press* 11 Jan 1942: 72. Print. Adapted from a *Parade* photographer's visit to the restaurant. He saw the chef prepare this dish and his pictures tell the story of Miller Brothers special recipe.

Crab Imperial - "Action Line." *Philadelphia Inquirer* 14 Aug 1971: 3. Print. Adapted from a recipe contributed by chef Sam Roggio of Miller Brothers.

Sea Food Lord Calvert - Maushard, Mary. "Chef savors memories: Miller Bros. gone, but not forgotten." *Evening Sun* (Baltimore) 11 Feb 1987: G1+. Print. Adapted a recipe contributed by chef Sam Roggio of Miller Brothers.

House of Welsh

Steaks "the old-fashioned House of Welsh way" - Adapted from D'Adamo, Joe. "House of Welsh long has been noted for sizzling steaks." *Evening Sun* (Baltimore) 4 Sept 1986: B13. Print.

Harvey House

Borscht - Adapted from D'Adamo, Joe. "Harvey House - 'a home away from home'." *Evening Sun* (Baltimore) 13 May 1982: 10. Print.

French Onion Soup, Calves Liver with Bacon and Homemade Rice Pudding - Adapted from Fogal, Gloria Jean. "Dinner for Six Features Favorite Dishes from Baltimore's Harvey House." *York Daily Record* 20 Sept 1987: 88. Print.

Jimmy Wu's New China Inn

Chicken Egg Drop Soup, Butterfly Shrimp and Beef Stir Fry with Tomato - "Chinese Food For Holidays." Baltimore Sun 20 Jan !966: B1. Print. Adapted from recipes contributed by Jimmy Wu, who adapted these for home use.

Thompson's Sea Girt House

Thompson's Crab Cakes - MacNees, James. "Maryland-Style Crab Cakes Make A Hit With Senators." *Baltimore Sun* 1 Feb 1963: 38+. Print. Adapted from a recipe contributed by George W. Thompson, Sr., owner of Thompson's Sea Girt House.

Thompson's Crab Fluffs- Jones, Carleton. "Casting the nets for crab fluff." *Baltimore Sun* 26 May 1982: C1+. Print. Adapted from a recipe contributed by chef Daniel Pacini of Thompson's Sea Girt House.

Rockfish Souffle and Oysters Florentine - Recipes compiled by the Maryland Dept. of Agriculture. *Maryland Seafood Cookbook II: Favorite Recipes from Maryland Chef's*. Annapolis: 1976. Print. Adapted from recipes contributed by Thompson's Sea Girt House.

Thompson's Shrimp Scampi - Adapted from a recipe compiled by Members and Friends of The Little Italy Lodge Order Sons of Italy In America. *Let's Cook Italian*. Baltimore: 1988-89. Print.

Brentwood Inn

Hot Buttered Rum - Williams, Lynn. "Mixing the Merriest Drinks." *Baltimore Sun* 18 Dec 1988: 1L+. Print. Adapted from a recipe contributed by John Czernikowski, Joe's son.

Hersh's Orchard Inn

Easy Gazpacho Soup - Adapted from D'Adamo, Joe. "Towson's Orchard knows how to please lots of customers." *Evening Sun* (Baltimore) 16 Feb 1984: 10. Print.

Crab Fritters with Curry Sauce - Ruhl, Sherrie. "Festive foods for parties." *Evening Sun* (Baltimore) 11 Dec 1991: F1-2. Print. Adapted from a recipe contributed by Hersh's Orchard Inn.

Hersh's Orchard Inn Orange Creamsicle - McGuire, Patrick A. "Cool Drinks from Area Restaurateurs." *Baltimore Sun/Sun Magazine* 28 July 1985: 8. Print. Adapted from a recipe contributed by Hersh's Orchard Inn.

Dici Naz Velleggia

Antipasto Caldo alla Velleggia and Saltimbocca alla Gino Marchetti - Adapted from recipes compiled by Members and Friends of the Little Italy Lodge Order Sons of Italy In America. *Let's Cook Italian*. Baltimore: 1988-89. Print.

Green Bean Salad - Adapted from Rapoport, Bonnie. *Dining In - Baltimore: A Collection of Gourmet Recipes for Complete Meals from Baltimore's Finest Restaurants*. Seattle: Peanut Butter Pub., 1981. Print.

Country Fare Inn

Tomatoes Mentonaisse, Scallops Gauguin and Cornish Game Hens - Adapted from Rapoport, Bonnie. *Dining In - Baltimore: A Collection of Gourmet Recipes for Complete Meals*. Seattle: Peanut Butter Pub., 1981. Print.

Le Canard au Poivre Vert (Roast Duck in Green Sauce) - Etter, Gerald. "Cookbook is also a guide to Maryland restaurants." *Baltimore Sun* 11 Jun 1986: 15E. Print. Adapted from a recipe contributed by Country Fare Inn.

Fiori

Fiori's Rice Croquettes and Marinara Sauce - Varkonyi, Charlyne. "A Genuine Cuisine." *Baltimore Sun* 14 Aug 1988: L1+. Print. Adapted from recipes contributed by Fiori.

House Salad and Fiori's Dressing - Adapted from Rapoport, Bonnie. *Dining In - Baltimore: A Collection of Gourmet Recipes for Complete Meals*. Seattle: Peanut Butter Pub., 1981. Print.

Fiori's Roquefort Dressing - O'Brien, Dawn and Rebecca Schenck. *Maryland's Historic Restaurants and their Recipes*. Winston-Salem: John F. Blair, Pub., 1995. Print.

Linguini with White Clam Sauce - Adapted from recipes compiled by Members and Friends of The Little Italy Lodge Order Sons of Italy In America. *Let's Cook Italian*. Baltimore: 1988-89. Print.

Pork Chops with Vinegar Peppers - Adapted from Maryland Chapter Arthritis Foundation. *Beyond Beer & Crabs*, Memphis: Wimmer Book Dist., 1982. Print.

Green Beans Margherita - Adapted from Rapoport, Bonnie. *Dining In - Baltimore: A Collection of Gourmet Recipes for Complete Meals*. Seattle: Peanut Butter Pub., 1981. Print.

Fiori's Chocolate Sabayon - Adapted from O'Brien, Dawn and Rebecca Schenck. *Maryland's Historic Restaurants and their Recipes*. Winston-Salem: John F. Blair, Pub., 1995. Print.

Italian Cheesecake - Adapted from a recipe compiled by Members and Friends of The Little Italy Lodge Order Sons of Italy In America. *Let's Cook Italian*. Baltimore: 1988-89. Print.

Milton Inn

"Paradise Lost" Oysters - Staff Report. "Oyster Cook-off prize given to Pa. woman." *Star-Democrat* (Easton, MD) 6 Jan 2006: A10. Print. Adapted from a recipe contributed by chef Brian Boston of Milton Inn.

Oyster Stew - Eskin, Leah. "Love Bites." *Baltimore Magazine* Feb 2007: 142-145. Print. Adapted from a recipe contributed by chef Brian Boston of Milton Inn.

Salade Eleanor - Adapted from O'Brien, Dawn and Rebecca Schenck. *Maryland's Historic Restaurants and their Recipes*. Winston-Salem: John F. Blair, Pub., 1995. Print.

Melini Veal Chop with White Bean Ragout - Adapted from Nunley, Debbie and Karen Jane Elliott. *A Taste of Maryland History: A Guide to Historic Eateries and Their Recipes*. Winston-Salem: John F. Blair, Pub., 2005. Print.

Pan-Fried Rockfish with Crab Hash and Delmarva Salsa - Sorgen, Carol. "Harvest Recipes." *Baltimore Sun* 12 Sept 1993: 13-15. Print. Adapted from a recipe contributed by chef Mark Henry of Milton Inn.

Blueberry Ketchup - Menzie, Karol V. "Some saucy ideas." *Daily Item* (Sunbury, PA) 17 Mar 1993: 12. Print. Adapted from a recipe contributed by chef Mark Henry of Milton Inn.

Cranberry Relish - Rom, Randi. "The Milton Inn's Cranberry Relish." Jmoreliving.com 31 Oct 2017. Jmoreliving.com/recipe/milton-inns-cranberry-relish/. Adapted from a recipe contributed by chef Brian Boston of Milton Inn.

Chocolate Marble Terrine - Clinton, Sherrie. "Holiday Desserts." *Evening Sun* (Baltimore) 20 Nov 1989: C10-11. Print. Adapted from a recipe contributed by chef Mark Henry of Milton Inn.

Raspberries with Lemon Curd in Meringue Shells - Varkonyi, Charlyne. "Pick A Blushing Dessert." *Baltimore Sun* 18 Jun 1989: 1N-4. Print. Adapted from a recipe contributed by chef Mark Henry of Milton Inn.

Rudys' 2900

Salmon Tartar - Morris, Linda Lowe. "An American success story from Germany." *Morning Call* (Allentown, PA) 20 Aug 1986: D3. Print. Adapted from a recipe contributed by Rudy Speckamp of Rudys' 2900.

Maryland Crabmeat Gumbo - Ercolano, Patrick. "When the kitchen gets hot, chef Dobbs starts cookin'." *Evening Sun* (Baltimore) 2 Mar 1988: G1+. Print. Adapted from a recipe contributed by chef Patrick Dobbs of Rudys' 2900.

Pumpkin Bisque with Ginger Crisp - Sorgen, Carol. "Fresh From the Garden." *Baltimore Sun* 27 Aug 1998: 14-15. Print. Adapted from a recipe contributed by chef Rudy Speckamp of Rudys' 2900.

Seafood Sanibel - Adapted from Baker, Mary Lou, and Bonnie Rapoport Marshall. *Dining In - Baltimore Cookbook Vol. II* Seattle: Peanut Butter Pub., 1988. Print.

Seared Rockfish with Oyster and Corn Stew - Sahler, Tracy. "Home Plate." *Daily Times* (Salisbury, MD) 5 Feb 2003: 13. Print. Adapted from a recipe contributed by the 2003 Rockfish Celebration first-place award winner, Rich Hoffman of Rudys' 2900.

Grouper and Salmon in Orange and Fennel Butter - Dorsey, John. "Chef's Secrets." *Baltimore Sun* 15 Sept 1985: A7-14. Print. Adapted from a recipe contributed by chef Rudy Speckamp of Rudys' 2900.

Soft Shell Crabs with Corn Relish, Field Greens and Roasted Red Pepper Sauce - Speckamp, Rudy. Season 1, Episode 5. Food Network Challenge; Challenge: Seafood Cook-Off. Food Network. www.foodnetwork.com/recipes/soft-shell-crabs-with-corn-relish-field-greens-and-roasted-red-pepper-sauce-recipe-2084893

Lobster Gratin With Green and White Asparagus - Shiver, Holly. "The Season the stalks and spears stand out." *Baltimore Sun* 23 Mar 2005: F1+. Print. Adapted from a recipe contributed by chef Rudy Speckamp of Rudys' 2900.

Boneless Breast of Pheasant Stuffed with Game Sausage in Apple Brandy Sauce - Adapted from Baker, Mary Lou, and Bonnie Rapoport Marshall. *Dining In - Baltimore Cookbook Vol. II* Seattle: Peanut Butter Pub., 1988. Print.

Fettucine Carbonara - Morris, Linda Lowe. "An American success story from Germany." *Morning Call* (Allentown, PA) 20 Aug 1986: D3. Print. Adapted from a recipe contributed by chef Rudy Speckamp of Rudys' 2900.

Roasted Parsnip Puree - Sorgen, Carol. "Fresh From the Garden." *Baltimore Sun* 27 Sept 1998: 14-15. Print. Adapted from a recipe contributed by chef Rudy Speckamp of Rudys' 2900.

Raspberries Romanoff - Adapted from Baker, Mary Lou, and Bonnie Rapoport Marshall. *Dining In - Baltimore Cookbook Vol.II* Seattle: Peanut Butter Pub., 1988. Print.

Pecan Diamonds - Compiled by the Cookbook Committee of St. Agnes Hospital Auxiliary. *Black-Eyed Susan Country: A Collection of Recipes* Memphis: Wimmer Book Dist., 1987. Print. Adapted from a recipe contributed by chef Rudy Speckamp of Rudys' 2900.

Crab Cooking Olympics

Gordon's of Orleans Street

Maryland Crab Cakes - Voltz, Jeanne. "Champion Crab Fare for Champion Crab Eaters," *Los Angeles Times*, 29 May 1969: 1+. Print. Adapted from a recipe contributed by chef Dave Gordon of Gordon's of Orleans Street.

Thompson's Sea Girt House

Imperial Crab á la Maryland - Ruffin, Cordelia. "Baltimore chef enters 'crab cooking Olympics'," *The Capitol* (Annapolis) 12 May 1970: 7. Print. Adapted from a recipe contributed by chef George W. (Tommy) Thompson, Jr. of the Sea Girt House.

Angelina's

Maryland Crab Cakes - Steiman, Harvey. "S. F. crab chefs feel the pinch of competition," *San Francisco Examiner* 24 Nov 1980: D2. Print. Adapted from a recipe contributed by chef Robert Reilly of Angelina's.

D'Adamo, Joe. ". . . and the winner is . . ." *Evening Sun* (Baltimore) 31 Dec 1981: 16. Print.

Crab Cioppino, Crab Louis, Deviled Crab, Crab Brendan, California Crab Cornets - Maushard, Mary. "Chef goes West to defend blue crabs, Baltimore," *Evening Sun* (Baltimore) 10 Feb 1982: D1-2. Print. Adapted from recipes contributed by chef Robert Reilly of Angelina's.

The Broadview

Crab Norfolk - Daniels, Hope. "From so-so to sublime: six hours of crab tasting," *Baltimore Sun* 10 Apr 1983: H1+. Print. Adapted from a recipe contributed by chef Paul Bartlett of the Broadv

Thank you for reading!

Dear Reader,

I hope you enjoyed *Dining Down Memory Lane, Volume II*. I have to tell you, I had so much fun researching and writing this book.

As an author, I love feedback. If you are so inclined, would you mind leaving a few words about this book on Amazon, Goodreads, or wherever you bought it? Reviews can be tough to come by these days, and this helps other readers decide if my book might be valuable to them.

Thank you so much for reading *Dining Down Memory Lane, Volume II* and for spending time with me.

In gratitude,

Shelley Howell

HEIDI MARIE BELL PHOTOGRAPHY

About the Author

Shelley Howell is a proud native Baltimorean with a passion for the past. She is the best-selling author of *Dining Down Memory Lane*, her debut book. A vintage enthusiast, her collection of recipes from now-defunct Baltimore restaurants is a treasure trove that will transport readers to another time and age. Shelley feels truly fortunate to have personally dined at most of these sorely missed establishments and wants to resurrect them here to share with you. An animal lover, Shelley lives in Towson and fosters orphaned kittens for the Maryland SPCA.

Shelleyhowellauthor.com

Facebook.com/shelleyhowellauthor